Message to the Motorist:  and READ

Safe and responsible driving begins with you! Be a safe driver and drive defensively. Being a defensive driver means bringing knowledge, skills and the right attitude to driving safely.

This study guide will teach you about traffic signs and traffic lights, pavement markings, traffic laws, safe driving, responsible driving, and what you need to know about driving a motorcycle so that you can increase your chances of getting your M1 licence. **Please note: the term motorcycle includes limited-speed motorcycles (LSMs) and three-wheeled motorcycles. It includes mopeds only where noted.**

This study guide includes over 300 sample test questions, numbered 1–301. Questions 1–201 are standard questions to help you practise for your G1 knowledge test. 40 of this type of question will be on the motorcycle knowledge test,

with an additional 20 questions specifically related to safe motorcycle driving. That's a total of 60 questions on your motorcycle knowledge test that you have to prepare for, so read and study all 301 questions in this guide.

For each question, select the most appropriate response, without looking below at the added information sections. These information boxes sometimes give the answer away. Other times they will provide you with valuable added information to help with your understanding.

While this study guide uses terms and language that are fairly easy to understand by the general public it is also highly recommended that you consult other sources for more detailed and specific information, such as:

- The Ontario Ministry of Transportation, www.mto.gov.on.ca

Note: Laws are constantly changing so obtain the most recent news from the Ministry of Transportation.

- Highway Traffic Act, www.e-laws.gov.on.ca
- Drive Test, www.drivetest.ca

It is also highly recommended that all new motorcycle drivers take a Ministry-approved motorcycle safety course to gain positive driving habits and learn and perfect the skills needed for safe and defensive driving.

Education, practice, commitment to safety, observing the rules and advice in this study guide and other sources will help you get and stay on the road safely.

Traffic Signs

1. a) No stopping.
    b) Stop if necessary and go when intersection is clear.
    c) Come to a full stop.
    d) Do not enter road.
    ⓘ If there is no stop line, crosswalk or sidewalk, stop at the intersection edge.	

2. a) You have the right-of-way.
    b) Give others the right-of-way.
    c) Always stop, then yield.
    d) Do not enter.
    ⓘ Traffic in the intersection or traffic close to it goes first. Only stop if necessary, then proceed when clear.	

3. a) School zone, reduce speed to 60 km/h.
    b) Slow down, school zone ahead, watch for children and drive with extra caution.
    c) You are approaching a school bus loading zone.
    d) Watch for pedestrians at crosswalk.
    ⓘ School zone signs are neon yellow or blue and 5-sided. Always reduce speed and watch for children.	

4. a) This is a pedestrian crosswalk.
    b) A railway crossing is X-shaped and filled in with red.
    c) Deer cross this area.
    d) A railway crossing sign indicating railway tracks cross the road.
    ⓘ Trains could be approaching so look both ways and be prepared to stop.	

5. a) No bicycles allowed.
   b) This is a bicycle route.
   c) School zone ahead.
   d) Do not watch for bicycles.

   ⓘ For everyone's safety bicycles are not allowed.

6. a) No parking anytime.
   b) Parking only allowed for longer than 30 minutes, 9 a.m.–6 p.m.
   c) You can only park after 5:00 p.m.
   d) Parking allowed for a maximum of 30 minutes within times posted.

   ⓘ This sign is usually in pairs or groups marking which areas you can park in.

7. a) Turn right only on a red light.
   b) No right turn ever.
   c) No right turn allowed on a red light.
   d) Do not enter.

   ⓘ If the traffic light is red at the intersection you may not turn right.

8. a) Enter.
   b) Do not enter road.
   c) Come to a complete stop.
   d) Only bicycles allowed.

   ⓘ Do not enter under any circumstance.

9. a) No wheelchair ramp.
    b) No parking at any time unless vehicle has a valid Accessible Parking Permit.
    c) No stopping at any time unless vehicle has a valid Accessible Parking Permit.
    d) No parking at any time.

    ⓘ You can only park in this area if your vehicle displays a valid Accessible Parking Permit.

10. a) Curb area reserved for picking up and dropping off people with disabilities.
    b) Curb area reserved for loading and unloading all passengers.
    c) Curb area reserved for vehicles parking with a valid permit.
    d) Curb area parking for all vehicles after 6:00 p.m.

    ⓘ Vehicles must display a valid Accessible Parking Permit in order to stop to load and unload people with disabilities.

11. a) No stopping.
    b) No parking.
    c) You may stand in the area between the signs.
    d) Bus stop is to the right and left.

    ⓘ Stopping is only allowed if loading or unloading passengers. This sign is used in groups or pairs.

12. a) No left turn.
    b) You may go in the opposite direction.
    c) No U-turn.
    d) Turning allowed after 6:00 p.m.

    ⓘ Do not turn around and go in the opposite direction.

13. a) No stopping except to unload passengers.
    b) There is a stop sign ahead.
    c) Come to a complete stop.
    d) No stopping at any time between the signs.

    ⓘ Besides no stopping, you are not allowed to load or unload passengers between signs that look like this.

14. a) No left turn during days and times posted.
    b) No left turn ever.
    c) Left turn allowed after 5:00 p.m.
    d) No left turn on Saturday or Sunday.

    ⓘ Carefully read the date and time as there is no left turn during days and times posted.

15. a) Parking allowed on either side of the signs.
    b) Parking available after 6:00 p.m.
    c) No parking allowed between the signs.
    d) There is parking available on either side of the arrows.

    ⓘ When used in pairs, there is no parking between the signs unless you are loading or unloading people or merchandise.

16. a) You are allowed to go straight through the intersection.
    b) You are not allowed to go straight through the intersection.
    c) You are not allowed to turn right or left.
    d) Stop at the intersection ahead.

    ⓘ You are not allowed to drive through the intersection so be prepared to turn.

17. a) You are approaching a school bus loading zone.
    b) Reduce speed to 40 km/h at all times.
    c) Reduce speed to 40 km/h when lights are flashing in this school zone.
    d) Watch for pedestrians at the crosswalk.

ⓘ The speed is lower during school hours when the yellow lights are flashing. School sign may be neon yellow or blue.

18. a) You are approaching a school zone crosswalk.
    b) You are entering a school zone.
    c) All vehicles must stop on the side of the road where the school bus is.
    d) All vehicles must stop for a school bus in all directions when lights are flashing.

ⓘ This sign is for multi-lane highways when there is no centre median divider.

19. a) There is an intersection ahead on the right.
    b) Stay to the left of the island.
    c) Stay to the right of the island.
    d) The road curves to the left for 1 km.

ⓘ There is a traffic island ahead and you must keep to the right of it.

20. a) The speed limit is 50 km/h.
    b) The speed limit is 50 km/h ahead.
    c) It is 50 km to the next rest area.
    d) The speed limit is 50 km/h for a distance of 50 km.

ⓘ The speed limit ahead is changing from what it is to 50 km/h.

21.   a) Reduce speed ahead.
      b) Exit to the right.
      c) One-way traffic in the direction indicated by the arrow.
      d) Two-way traffic permitted.

ⓘ You can only travel in the direction of the arrow.

22.   a) No pedestrians allowed on roadway.
      b) Pedestrians may not cross the road.
      c) There is no crosswalk in the area.
      d) Do not enter—construction zone.

ⓘ Pedestrians are not allowed on the road.

23.   a) No passing on this road.
      b) You may pass on this road.
      c) Two-way traffic ahead.
      d) Do not enter.

ⓘ For safety reasons there is no passing on this roadway.

24.   a) Right turn and passing lane ahead.
      b) Keep to the right except when passing on two-way road sections.
      c) Road turns to the right.
      d) Merge ahead.

ⓘ You are permitted to pass on the left; otherwise, keep to the right.

Traffic Signs

25. a) Stop and yield right-of-way to pedestrians at crosswalk. Do not pass from sign to crossing.
    b) Railroad crossing ahead, no pedestrians allowed.
    c) Pedestrians or vehicles may not enter the roadway.
    d) Deer crossing ahead.

    ⓘ You are approaching a pedestrian crosswalk. Slow down, yield to pedestrians and be prepared to stop.

26. a) If you are in lanes 1, 2 or 3 you must only go in the direction of that lane's arrow.
    b) If you are in lane 1 you may go straight and left.
    c) If you are in lane 2 you may go in any direction.
    d) If you are in lane 3, you may go straight or turn right.

    ⓘ These signs are either painted on the roadway or hung above at intersections. They tell drivers the direction they must travel for the lane they are in.

❶ ❷ ❸

27. a) Lane is not for left turns.
    b) Lane is only for two-way left turns.
    c) Turn left or right.
    d) No U-turn.

    ⓘ This sign can be above the ground or on the road which means two-way left turns only.

Driving Tips for All Seasons   April showers bring...**Puddles**

Heavy rain may pool on streets where the road is uneven or, worse, where there is a pothole. Avoid damage to your vehicle by slowing down in and around puddles.

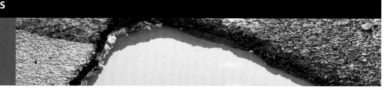

28. a) Lanes are for pedestrians only, no vehicles permitted during days and times posted.

    b) Lanes are for loading and unloading passengers only during days and times posted.

    c) Lanes are for 5 or more passengers during days and times posted.

    d) Lanes are for 3 or more passengers in the vehicles shown, plus bicycles, during the days and times shown or all the time (depending on the sign).

ⓘ These lanes are for bicycles or specific vehicles that carry 3 or more people, for the times indicated or all the time if no time is shown.

2 or More Persons

ⓘ HOV or High Occupancy Vehicle lanes are for a driver and one or more passengers. Sometimes the number required is specifically indicated such as in the sign at left. The purpose of HOV lanes is to promote carpooling and using buses to reduce congestion and emissions and improve air quality.

29. a) No passing.

    b) No passing except to enter HOV lanes.

    c) Do not cross lanes, sidewalk ahead.

    d) Do not cross into or out of HOV lanes for area shown.

ⓘ You can not change lanes into or out of the HOV lanes.

Do Not Cross

30. a) Crosswalk ahead, watch for pedestrians crossing.
    b) Intersection ahead, direction of arrow indicates who has right-of-way.
    c) Railroad crossing ahead.
    d) Quiet, church zone ahead.

    (i) When approaching an intersection with this sign the direction of the arrow indicates who has right-of-way.

31. a) Hidden left turn ahead.
    b) Hidden crosswalk ahead.
    c) There is a three-way stop ahead that is hidden.
    d) There is a hidden road ahead.

    (i) Drivers on the hidden road ahead may not see traffic from the main road when they reach the intersection.

32. a) The road narrows ahead.
    b) The two-way road curves ahead.
    c) A narrow bridge ahead.
    d) Slower traffic move to the right.

    (i) This symbol represents a bridge and that the bridge is narrower than the roadway.

33. a) There is a narrow bridge ahead.
    b) The road narrows ahead.
    c) Two-lane roadway ends.
    d) Merge with oncoming traffic.

    (i) The pavement will become narrower ahead.

10

34. a) The road bends to the right ahead.
    b) The road bends to the left ahead.
    c) One-way traffic ahead.
    d) Right-turn-only lane ahead.

    ⓘ Adjust driving accordingly as the road bends or curves slightly to the right.

35. a) One lane ahead.
    b) No turns ahead.
    c) The road branches off ahead.
    d) There is a three-way stop ahead.

    ⓘ The road divides ahead. Slow down in case you or others have to turn off the main roadway.

36. a) Exit to the right.
    b) Sharp turn here.
    c) Crosswalk ahead.
    d) Railway crossing.

    ⓘ These arrowheads are called chevrons. They warn you about sharp turns and are posted in groups to guide drivers.

37. a) Winding road ahead.
    b) Hidden intersection ahead.
    c) Turn right at bridge ahead.
    d) Road turns or bends to the right sharply ahead.

    ⓘ The road changes and bends sharply so reduce speed in order to follow the roadway safely.

38. a) Intersection ahead.
     b) Stop sign ahead.
     c) Stop at crosswalk ahead.
     d) School children crossing ahead.

(i) There is a stop sign ahead so slow down.

39. a) Truck weigh station ahead.
     b) Sharp turn ahead.
     c) Hazard close to edge of road.
     d) Single lane ahead.

(i) An island or something close to the road is a hazard. Downward lines indicate side to pass hazard on.

40. a) Slower traffic keep to the right.
     b) Highway ends ahead.
     c) The two-way road ahead is split with a median.
     d) Merge with traffic ahead.

(i) The two-way road ahead will be split with a median. Each side of the road is one-way traffic.

41. a) Bridge ahead.
     b) Gravel road ahead.
     c) The two-way road ahead is not divided with a median.
     d) The two-way road ahead is divided with a median.

(i) You will be required to share the road ahead with oncoming traffic. The road will not be divided by a median.

42. a) A winding road is ahead.
     b) Sharp turn in the road ahead.
     c) Hazard to the right.
     d) Hazard to the left.

 The road is winding ahead which may obstruct your ability to see other vehicles.

43. a) Bridge ices.
     b) Slippery when wet.
     c) You are entering a snowbelt area.
     d) Winding road ahead.

 The road is slippery when wet. Reduce speed and drive with caution.

44. a) Road has a bend to the right.
     b) Road turns sharply to the right.
     c) Left lane ends ahead.
     d) Right lane ends ahead.

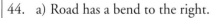 The right lane ends ahead and you are required to merge with traffic in the lane to the left if you are in the right lane.

45. a) No bicycles allowed.
     b) Official bicycle route.
     c) School zone ahead.
     d) Bicycle crossing ahead.

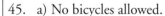 Bicycle crossing ahead so slow down and proceed with caution.

13

46. a) Broken bridge ahead.
     b) Bridge ices ahead.
     c) Bridge lifts ahead to let boats pass.
     d) Do not drive on bridge ahead.

ⓘ The bridge ahead will lift or swing up to let boats pass.

47. a) Paved road ends ahead.
     b) Gravel road ends ahead.
     c) One-way road ahead.
     d) Road ends ahead.

ⓘ The paved road ends ahead and is replaced by a gravel road. Reduce speed accordingly.

48. a) Hidden intersection ahead.
     b) Two-lane highway begins.
     c) Two lanes will merge to one. Driver on the right has right-of-way.
     d) Two lanes will merge to one. Drivers in both lanes are responsible to merge safely.

ⓘ Two lanes are merging into one. Merging is the equal responsibility of drivers in both lanes.

49. a) Divided highway begins.
     b) Divided highway ends.
     c) Slower traffic keep to the right.
     d) No intersection ahead.

ⓘ Traffic goes in both directions ahead so stay on the right.

50. a) Snowmobiles cross this roadway.
     b) Only snowmobiles allowed in area.
     c) Provincial park area.
     d) Snowmobiles may not enter.

ⓘ Snowmobiles cross this area so drive cautiously as you may not see them.

51. a) Warning—construction zone ahead.
     b) Sharp turn ahead in the direction of the arrow.
     c) Road is very bumpy ahead.
     d) Road closed ahead.

ⓘ The checkered board pattern warns of danger so slow down and proceed with caution in the direction of the arrow.

52. a) No animals allowed.
     b) Deer may cross the road.
     c) You are entering a game farm.
     d) Watch for deer hunters.

ⓘ Deer may cross the road in this area. Slow down and be aware of your surroundings.

53. a) Construction zone ahead.
     b) Railroad crossing ahead.
     c) Traffic lights ahead.
     d) City zone ahead.

ⓘ You will be approaching a traffic light ahead. Slow down as you may have to stop.

54. a) There is a steep hill ahead.
    b) You are in a mountain zone.
    c) Caution, trucks turning.
    d) Construction zone ahead.

    ℹ️ The road has a steep hill ahead. Slow down and be prepared to shift into a lower gear to slow down your vehicle.

55. a) Trucks may approach the road from the right.
    b) Trucks may approach the road from the left.
    c) Construction zone.
    d) No trucks allowed on road.

    ℹ️ Truck entrance is on the side of the road where truck is shown, in this case on the right.

56. a) The road ends in 3.9 km.
    b) Only vehicles over 3.9 m permitted ahead.
    c) There is a maximum 3.9 m clearance ahead on the overpass.
    d) Divided highway ends in 3.9 km.

    ℹ️ If driving a tall vehicle you may not be able to pass. Take note of clearances before approaching underpasses.

57. a) Men at work ahead.
    b) Pedestrian crossing ahead.
    c) School zone ahead.
    d) Share the road with pedestrians.

    ℹ️ Watch for pedestrians as the roadway is meant to be shared. Drive cautiously.

58. a) Watch out for fallen rocks.
    b) Steep hill, shift into lower gear.
    c) Construction zone ahead.
    d) Large hail stone area.

ⓘ Rocks could be falling so drive carefully and be prepared to avoid a collision.

59. a) Railroad tracks ahead.
    b) Hospital ahead, keep quiet and watch for ambulances.
    c) School crossing ahead.
    d) You are approaching a hidden school bus stop.

ⓘ Be very cautious, watch for children and be prepared to stop for a school bus with flashing red lights.

60. a) School crossing or school crossing ahead.
    b) Hidden school bus stop ahead.
    c) Children must be accompanied by an adult in this area.
    d) Intersection ahead.

ⓘ Watch for children crossing and follow the direction of the crossing guard. These signs may be neon yellow or blue.

61. a) There is winding road for 50 km.
    b) Maximum safe speed to drive on ramp is 50 km/h.
    c) Drive at least 50 km on ramp.
    d) Next rest stop is in 50 km.

ⓘ All ramps have a maximum safe speed you can travel. Obey these maximums.

62. a) Bridge ahead.
    b) Bridge ices.
    c) Road may have water flowing over it.
    d) Road ends at lake.

ⓘ Some roads are near high water areas where the road may get covered with water. Reduce speed and drive carefully.

63. a) Mountain zone ahead.
    b) Bumpy or uneven road ahead.
    c) Construction zone ahead.
    d) Falling rocks ahead.

ⓘ Slow down and keep both hands on the steering wheel for best control of your vehicle and to avoid sudden shifts.

64. a) Survey crew working on road.
    b) Road closed ahead.
    c) 1 km construction zone begins.
    d) Construction zone begins in 1 km.

ⓘ Road speed, curve and terrain may change in construction zone ahead. Slow down and drive cautiously.

65. a) Person controlling traffic ahead.
    b) Roadwork ahead.
    c) Survey crew assessing road ahead.
    d) Construction zone ahead.

ⓘ Slow down and pay attention to instructions from the traffic control person ahead.

66. a) Movie filming set.
   b) Sightseeing binoculars ahead.
   c) Survey crew ahead.
   d) Bird watchers ahead.

(i) Surveyors often have to measure land in new areas. Use caution as surveyors may be near the road.

67. a) Fallen rock ahead.
   b) Snow removal ahead.
   c) Road work occurring ahead.
   d) Sand quarry ahead.

(i) Reduce speed, drive with caution and watch for construction personnel working on the road ahead.

68. a) There is a temporary detour from the normal traffic roadway.
   b) Be prepared to drive around mountains ahead.
   c) Downward sloping hill ahead.
   d) Closed lane ahead.

(i) The road detours temporarily from what it usually is due to road work.

69. a) Reduce speed. You are entering the construction zone.
   b) Construction zone begins in 1 km.
   c) Worker ahead surveying the land.
   d) Gravel road ahead.

(i) It is very important to obey the posted speed limits in construction zones as fines may be doubled.

70. a) Golf course ahead.

    b) Fallen rocks ahead.

    c) Provincial camp ground ahead.

    d) There are grooves in the pavement.

    ⓘ The pavement has been grooved so you may not be able to stop easily. Obey all posted speed limits for this area.

71. a) Right turn lane only ahead.

    b) Lane is closed. Move into lane directed by arrow and merge with traffic.

    c) Lane is open. Adjust speed for construction zone.

    d) Hidden intersection ahead on right.

    ⓘ Reduce your speed when merging with traffic in the lane shown by the arrow.

72. a) Bridge narrows ahead.

    b) Bridge ahead.

    c) Third lane begins.

    d) Lane ends and is closed for roadwork.

    ⓘ Lane ahead is closed and you must merge with traffic in the lane that is open. Obey all posted speed limits.

73. a) Winding road ahead.

    b) Follow the road in the direction shown.

    c) Watch for farm vehicles approaching from the left.

    d) Construction zone begins to the left.

    ⓘ Always follow the arrows with flashing lights as they indicate which direction to follow.

74. a) Stop and drive slowly through campground.
    b) Obey the crossing guard with the signs they hold up.
    c) Slow down and be prepared to stop.
    d) Slow down, stop and exit the construction zone.

    ⓘ These signs may be held by road work personnel. Drive slowly and be prepared to stop.

75. a) Pass the pace vehicle only when you see this sign flashing.
    b) Do not pass the pace vehicle that has this sign flashing.
    c) Pass only to the left.
    d) Pass only to the right.

    ⓘ Do not pass vehicles with this flashing sign.

76. a) The road detours so follow this sign until you come to the regular road.
    b) Follow the detour marker only if you choose not to take the regular road.
    c) Merge with road that closed.
    d) Lane closed ahead. Slow down and merge with traffic.

    ⓘ Follow this sign through the detour until you come to the regular road.

 FOLLOW

Driving Tips for All Seasons   **Stay hydrated**

Keep cool water with you when travelling on hot summer days, even for short distances. Construction, which is very common in summer, can delay you considerably. Do not let yourself dehydrate.

Information and Direction Signs

77. a) An exit sign telling you which lane to drive in if you want to exit to Bradley Street. b) Two right lanes must exit to Bradley Street. c) Only the right lane exits to Bradley Street. d) No left turns on Bradley Street. ⓘ Exit signs indicate which lane to drive in if you want to exit or if you want to stay on the main road.	Bradley Street ↱↱
78. a) A highway exit is coming up in 20 km. b) A highway exit is coming up in 10 km. c) An advance exit sign telling you which lanes go off the highway. d) An advance exit sign telling you 2 right lanes do not exit off the highway. ⓘ Advance signs are also used with exit signs. Ensure you are in the correct lane to exit a highway.	Ontario Street ↱↗ EXIT
79. a) Indicates which direction to go for the city or town posted. b) All towns or cities posted on this sign are 50 km away. c) Construction ahead so be prepared to detour by direction shown. d) Indicates there is provincial park in the city or town posted. ⓘ This direction and information sign tells you which direction to travel to get to the city or town posted.	↑ LINDSAY ← OSHAWA PORT HOPE →
80. a) Indicates which direction to go for the city or town posted. b) Indicates distance, in kilometres, to the city or town posted. c) Indicates the distance to campgrounds and green conservation areas. d) Indicates by distance shown that Guelph is before Hamilton. ⓘ Sign tells you the distance, in kilometres, from the city or town posted. Helps with rest stops and gas planning.	HAMILTON 70 GUELPH 99

81. a) One left lane exits off the highway.
    b) Two left lanes exit off the highway.
    c) Right lane only exits off the highway.
    d) One or more lanes allow you to exit off the highway.

    ⓘ Advance signs indicate which lanes exit off the highway, by the yellow boxed "exit" notation.

82. a) To get to the Q.E.W. go by way of the 403.
    b) Both the Q.E.W. and the 401 are coming up on the right.
    c) The Q.E.W. is coming up on the right.
    d) The 401 is coming up on the right.

    ⓘ Highways are connected and in this case you get to the Q.E.W. by way of (via) the 403.

83. a) Interchange 346 is 346 km from Toronto.
    b) It is 34.6 km to Dixie Rd.
    c) You will be approaching interchange 346 in 1 km.
    d) You will be approaching the Dixie Rd. exit in 346 km.

    ⓘ Highway 401 begins in Windsor so interchange 346, Dixie Rd., is 346 km from Windsor.

84. a) Traffic bulletin signs change with updates on traffic, delays and lane closures.
    b) Traffic bulletin signs post the same information on traffic, delays and lane closures.
    c) Informs drivers about next exits.
    d) Informs drivers about nearby parks and recreation information.

    ⓘ These signs inform drivers about current driving conditions so that alternate routes can be taken.

85. a) Airplane parking area.
    b) Route to airport.
    c) Route to airplane production.
    d) Indicates you are under a fly zone.

ⓘ Follow these signs to get to an airport.

86. a) Boat docking route.
    b) Deep water ahead.
    c) Ferry service route.
    d) No public swimming ahead.

ⓘ Follow these signs to get to a ferry service.

87. a) Indicates there are police, a hospital, an information desk and an airport in one building.
    b) Indicates there is only an airport nearby.
    c) Shows what services and facilities are not available nearby or off-road.
    d) Shows what services and facilities are located nearby or off-road.

ⓘ Indicates what services and facilities are available off the road. Other services can include car pool lots, universities, etc.

88. a) Wheelchair parking only.
    b) Indicates facilities accessible by wheelchair.
    c) Indicates retirement living community. Slow down and keep noise low.
    d) Indicates there is a hospital nearby.

ⓘ Indicates there are ramps and other wheelchair accessible facilities.

89. a) Railroad crossing ahead.
    b) Train maintenance area.
    c) Route to cargo railway station.
    d) Route to passenger railway station.

    ⓘ Indicates route to where passengers can be met or dropped off at the railway station.

90. a) Speed in area is very slow, less than 40 km/h.
    b) Slow-moving vehicle on road, travelling less than 40 km/h.
    c) Snow removal vehicle ahead.
    d) Danger, keep out, road under construction.

    ⓘ All vehicles moving less than 40 km/hr must display a slow-moving vehicle sign at rear if driving on a road.

91. a) Bilingual signs are for educational purposes only.
    b) Bilingual signs are posted near French schools for you to follow.
    c) Obey bilingual sign only if you read and speak French.
    d) Bilingual signs provide important information. Read message in language understood best.

    ⓘ Bilingual signs have two languages on one sign. Sometimes, there may be two signs, one English and one French.

92. a) Two exits exist for Bowesville Road.
    b) Only exit onto Bowesville Road if you drive an emergency vehicle.
    c) Numbers at the bottom assist emergency vehicles to plan best routes.
    d) Some information signs have numbers at the bottom to assist you with exits and distances.

    ⓘ The numbering system at the bottom of some signs is to help emergency vehicles plan the best route.

93. **When are you required to wear a seatbelt?**
    a) Wearing a seatbelt is optional.
    b) Only drivers are required to wear a seatbelt.
    c) Only passengers are required to wear a seatbelt.
    d) All drivers and passengers are required to wear a seatbelt and be properly buckled up.

    ⓘ Drivers will receive a fine and demerit points for not wearing a seatbelt. Drivers must ensure all passengers under the age of 16 are properly buckled up. Unbuckled passengers 16 years and older can be fined.

94. **What does the law state about seatbelts and children 9–18 kg (20–40lbs)?**
    a) All infants, toddlers and children under 8 must be in a booster seat.
    b) All infants, toddlers and children under 8 must be in a rear-facing child car seat.
    c) All infants, toddlers and children under 8 must wear protective head gear.
    d) All toddlers 9–18 kg must be in an approved child car seat that is properly attached.

    ⓘ A child's weight and/or age determines what type of car seat is required. It is important that all child car seats meet safety standards and are properly secured.

95. **How far away must headlights and rear lights be seen?**
    a) From 50 m away.
    b) From 150 m away.
    c) From 1150 m away.
    d) They must be seen clearly in the dark.

    ⓘ You must also have your rear licence plate illuminated with white lighting when headlights are on. Ensure headlights are on 1/2 an hour before sunset and leave them on for 1/2 an hour after sunrise.

96. **When using highbeam lights when do you have to switch to lowbeam lights?**
    a) Within 150 m of oncoming vehicles.
    b) Within 50 m of oncoming vehicles.
    c) You do not have to switch.
    d) If the oncoming car puts their highbeams on you do not have to switch.

    ⓘ Use lowbeam lights when you are less than 60 m behind another vehicle and within 150 m of oncoming vehicles. Never use parking lights for driving. They are only for parking.

97. **Why must your vehicle undergo emissions testing?**
    a) To identify if it's grossly polluting the environment.
    b) Your vehicle may be of an age where it's necessary to get tested.
    c) So that you may renew your vehicle registration.
    d) All of the above.

    ⓘ If you receive notice to get emissions testing, your car must pass in order to get a renewal sticker so that you may drive your vehicle.

98. **Why must you use signals when turning?**
    a) To inform other drivers of what you want to do.
    b) To inform pedestrians of what you want to do.
    c) To send out an alert of your intentions.
    d) All of the above.

    ⓘ Failing to use proper signals can result in a fine and demerit points. Always signal to inform others of your intention. Follow all rules for turning.

99. Unless posted in cities, towns, villages and built-up areas the maximum speed limit is?…

a) 40 km/h.

b) 50 km/h.

c) 70 km/h.

d) 80 km/h.

ⓘ Where no speed limit is posted, the limit is 80 km/h outside these areas.

100. What are you required to do if a police officer signals you to pull over?

a) Slow down, safely pull over in the left lane and come to a complete stop.

b) Slow down, safely pull over in the right lane and come to a complete stop.

c) Slow down and stop in the lane you are in.

d) Signal and stop at the next intersection and wait for the police officer.

ⓘ Do not get out of your vehicle. Wait for the police officer to come to you.

101. How much time do you have to surrender your licence, vehicle permit (or copy) and insurance when asked by a police officer?

a) Immediately.

b) Within 12 hours.

c) Within 24 hours.

d) You do not have to, they will look you up in the system.

ⓘ You must present these required documents immediately. Failure to do so can result in a fine.

102. **How much space should you have between you and any vehicle you are following?**
   a) No rule applies and you will not get a fine or demerit points as long as caution is used.
   b) There is a rule of 20 seconds but it is for motorcycle drivers only.
   c) At least 12 seconds so you can see around the vehicle ahead and also have enough time to stop.
   d) At least 2 seconds so you can see around the vehicle ahead and also have enough time to stop.

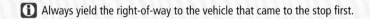 If driving conditions are not ideal add more space especially if driving in bad weather or following larger vehicles, motorcycles, or when you have a heavy load. Use markers on the road to help determine correct following distance.

103. **If 3 vehicles are at an all-way stop, who has the right-of-way?**
   a) The vehicle that got there first.
   b) The vehicle on the left.
   c) The vehicle turning right.
   d) The vehicle turning left.

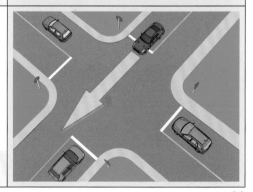

Always yield the right-of-way to the vehicle that came to the stop first.

104. **If 2 vehicles come to an uncontrolled intersection at the same time, who has the right-of-way?**
    a) The vehicle on the right.
    b) The vehicle on the left.
    c) The vehicle turning right.
    d) The vehicle turning left.

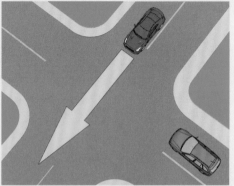

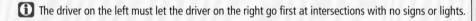 The driver on the left must let the driver on the right go first at intersections with no signs or lights.

105. **If you are turning left at an uncontrolled intersection and a pedestrian is crossing your path, who has the right-of-way?**
    a) You do. Come to a complete stop and make your turn.
    b) Any other car at the intersection that is turning right.
    c) You must yield the right-of-way to approaching traffic and/or to pedestrians crossing.
    d) Whoever is more in a hurry goes first.

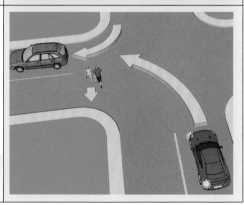

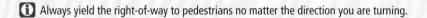 Always yield the right-of-way to pedestrians no matter the direction you are turning.

106. **If you approach an intersection on a main road that is blocked with traffic, what should you do?**
   a) Stop before entering the intersection.
   b) Move up so cars behind you can move forward.
   c) Slowly proceed through the intersection.
   d) Turn left or right to avoid the heavy traffic back-up.

ⓘ Only proceed after stopping and when the way is clear. Do not allow yourself to be stuck in the intersection as the light turns red.

107. **How much room do cyclists need on either side of themselves as a safety zone?**
   a) 4 m.
   b) 3 m.
   c) 2 m.
   d) 1 m.

ⓘ Ensure you share the road with all vehicles, including cyclists. If the lane is too narrow to share, change lanes.

31

108. What challenges do commercial vehicles have that are dangerous for other vehicles?
- a) They have small blind spots.
- b) They make wide turns.
- c) They roll forward after stopping.
- d) They block large amounts of snow and slush from your windshield.

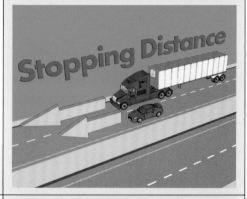

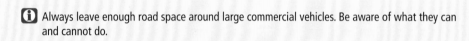 Always leave enough road space around large commercial vehicles. Be aware of what they can and cannot do.

109. Coming to a complete stop at an intersection is required, but where do you stop if there is no stop line, crosswalk or sidewalk?
- a) You stop right beside the stop sign.
- b) You stop right before the stop sign.
- c) You stop at the edge of the intersection.
- d) You stop a little into the intersection so that you can see traffic and pedestrians.

 You must also wait for the intersection to clear before entering it.

110. **When do you stop for school buses if there is a median?**
   a) Whenever you approach and see one.
   b) Never, because they will stop for you.
   c) Whenever they stop.
   d) Only if you are behind a stopped bus which has its upper red alternating lights flashing.

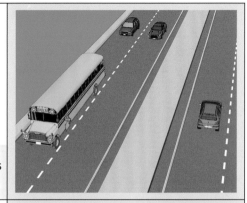

ⓘ School buses also have flashing stop signs that swing out from the driver's side, notifying vehicles to stop. Stay back the required distance.

111. **If there is no median, how far in front and behind a school bus are you required to stop when its lights are flashing?**
   a) At least 20 m behind and far enough in front for children to exit the bus and cross safely.
   b) At least 20 ft behind and far enough in front for children to exit the bus and cross safely.
   c) At least 10 m behind and far enough in front for children to exit the bus and cross safely.
   d) At least 10 ft behind and far enough in front for children to exit the bus and cross safely.

ⓘ Only proceed when the bus lights have stopped flashing or the bus has moved.

112. **When you come to a railway crossing and there are flashing signal lights, what must you do?**

    a) Continue slowly because flashing lights are only a warning to drive slow.

    b) Stop and then proceed slowly across the tracks.

    c) Stop and wait for the signal lights to stop flashing.

    d) Drive around the gate or barrier to avoid getting stuck on the tracks.

    ⓘ Stop at least 5 m back from the nearest rail, gate or barrier. Only cross tracks once gates rise and lights stop flashing.

113. **It is illegal to not stop behind a stopped school bus with alternating flashing red lights. If you do not stop what can happen?**

    a) You can be fined $40–$200.

    b) You can be fined $400–$2,000.

    c) You can be fined $4,000–$20,000.

    d) You will not be fined for the first offence; you will only receive a warning.

    ⓘ You can get 6 demerit points for a first offence and a fine of $400–$2,000. You may also face a 30-day licence suspension.

114. **You must share the road with motorcycles, cyclists, commercial vehicles, pedestrians, farm machinery and buses.**

    a) The above statement is false.

    b) The above statement is true.

    c) All of the above are correct except for farm machinery.

    d) All of the above are correct except for pedestrians because they are not in a vehicle.

    ⓘ You must share the road with all vehicles and pedestrians. Failing to do so can result in a fine and demerit points.

115. **Can you make a right turn on a red light?**
    a) Yes, after coming to a complete stop and as long as a sign does not tell you otherwise.
    b) Yes, as long as you are in an HOV lane.
    c) No, there are no right turns on red lights allowed in Ontario.
    d) No, there are no right turns on roadways shared with pedestrians.

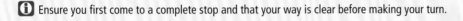 Ensure you first come to a complete stop and that your way is clear before making your turn.

116. **How do you make a left turn from a two-way road onto a two-way road?**
    a) Turn from the right lane making a smooth arc into the right curb lane.
    b) Turn from the right lane making a smooth arc into the lane right of the centre line.
    c) Turn from the closest lane to the centre dividing line into the right curb lane.
    d) Turn from the closest lane to the centre dividing line making a smooth arc into the lane to the right of the centre dividing line.

Unless otherwise posted left turns are made from the far left lane. Signal, check all directions and ensure way is clear. After turning move into the right curb lane when it is clear to do so.

117. How do you make a left turn from a two-way road onto a two lane one-way road?

    a) Turn from the far left lane into the left curb lane.

    b) Turn from the far left lane into the right curb lane.

    c) Turn from the far right lane into the left curb lane.

    d) Turn from the right lane into the right curb lane.

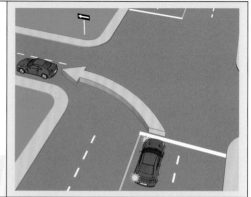

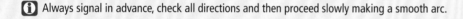 Always signal in advance, check all directions and then proceed slowly making a smooth arc.

118. Why is it a bad idea to turn your steering wheel to the left while waiting to make a left turn at an intersection?

    a) In case you need to turn right—it will be harder to steer out of the turn.

    b) It is not a bad idea—your vehicle will not be able to make the turn in time if you do not.

    c) Another vehicle can push your vehicle into oncoming traffic.

    d) Turning your steering wheel unnecessarily will add to your car's wear and tear.

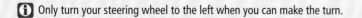 Only turn your steering wheel to the left when you can make the turn.

119. **What do the markings on the road mean and what does the sign represent in the picture?**

    a) There is a left turn lane in the centre for those travelling north.

    b) There is a left turn lane in the centre for those travelling south.

    c) There is an extra lane for driving in.

    d) There is a two-way left turn lane in the centre for traffic going in both directions.

ⓘ Signal and move into the left turn lane. Make your turn carefully and only when the way is clear.

120. **Can you turn left on a red light from a one-way road onto a one-way road?**

    a) Yes, if you signal, stop first in the farthest left lane and then proceed when the way is clear.

    b) Yes, as long as you drive slowly and cautiously.

    c) No left turns are permitted on a red light in Ontario.

    d) Left turns are only permitted from two-way roads to two-way roads on a green light.

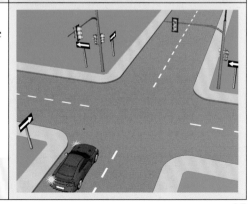

ⓘ Ensure you yield to pedestrians and traffic after first coming to a complete stop.

121. To make a U-turn you must be able to see how far in both directions?
- a) 50 m.
- b) 100 m.
- c) 150 m.
- d) 200 m.

ⓘ Never make a U-turn on a curve, hill, railway crossing, bridge, tunnel or where your view is blocked. It is illegal to do so.

122. When can you remove your seatbelt while driving?
- a) When you are backing up.
- b) When you are the only person in the car.
- c) If you are a G1 driver.
- d) If you are on a country road.

ⓘ To see properly while backing up you can remove your seatbelt to turn your body. Remember to put it back on as soon as you move forward.

123. When parking uphill with a curb what should you do?
- a) Turn your tires to the left to catch the curb if your vehicle rolls backward.
- b) Turn your tires to the right to catch the curb if your vehicle rolls backward.
- c) Make your tires straight and parallel with the curb.
- d) The direction of your tires does not matter as long as you set the parking brake.

ⓘ Turn your tires to the left and set your parking brake. Always do both.

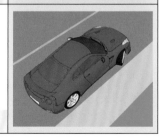

124. **Who has the right-of-way in a roundabout?**
   a) Traffic approaching the roundabout.
   b) Traffic in the roundabout.
   c) Traffic turning right in the roundabout.
   d) Traffic turning left in the roundabout.

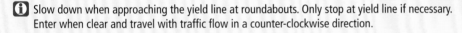 Slow down when approaching the yield line at roundabouts. Only stop at yield line if necessary. Enter when clear and travel with traffic flow in a counter-clockwise direction.

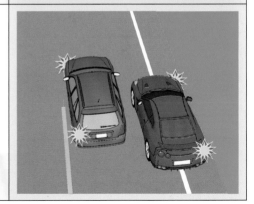

125. **When can you pass on a shoulder?**
   a) Only if a vehicle is turning left and you have an unpaved shoulder on the right.
   b) Only if a vehicle is turning left and you have a paved shoulder on the right.
   c) Whenever the vehicle in front of you is moving under 40 km/h.
   d) Whenever you can do so safely.

ⓘ Passing is generally done from the left but you can pass on the right in this case if there is another vehicle turning left and only if the shoulder is paved.

126. **Two solid yellow painted lines on a roadway as in this diagram do which of the following?**
    a) Help in calculating distances from one exit to the next.
    b) Act as left and right turn lane markings.
    c) Provide drivers information about upcoming exits.
    d) Are warnings to guide drivers away from fixed obstacles like islands, bridges etc.

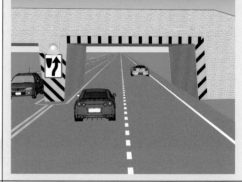

ⓘ Steer clear of solid painted road markings that are around fixed objects to avoid a collision.

127. **What do double solid pavement markings mean?**
    a) Vehicles travelling on the right may pass when the way is clear.
    b) Vehicles travelling on the left may pass when the way is clear.
    c) Both vehicles may pass in either direction when the way is clear.
    d) No vehicles may pass in either direction.

ⓘ Solid yellow lines divide traffic going in opposite directions and do not allow vehicles to pass in either direction.

128. **What must you do when changing lanes?**
   a) Check mirrors and blind spots for space, signal, check for space again, steer into lane.
   b) Signal and steer into lane slowly.
   c) Signal and steer into lane quickly to get into lane safely.
   d) Sound horn, signal and move slowly.

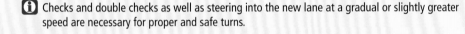 Checks and double checks as well as steering into the new lane at a gradual or slightly greater speed are necessary for proper and safe turns.

129. **At a pedestrian crossing, you should not pass cars within how many metres from the crossing?**
   a) 3 m.
   b) 30 m.
   c) 300 m.
   d) 30 000 m.

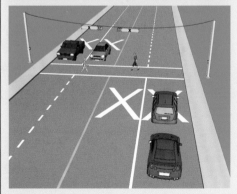

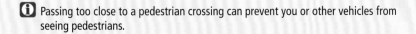 Passing too close to a pedestrian crossing can prevent you or other vehicles from seeing pedestrians.

130. **What are passing or climbing lanes for?**

    a) They allow for frequent stops and a rest area ahead.

    b) They are for vehicles that have trouble climbing hills.

    c) They help thin out traffic by providing an extra lane.

    d) They allow slower vehicles to move into the right lane so faster ones can pass on the left.

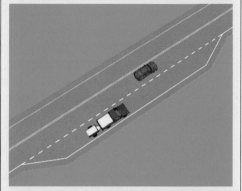

ⓘ Advance notice of passing lanes is provided as are signs warning when these lanes end. If driving at a reduced speed, move into the right lane and allow faster moving vehicles to pass. Merge safely back when passing lane ends.

131. **When can you pass on the right?**

    a) You may never pass on the right.

    b) You can only pass on the right if there is an emergency.

    c) On one-way or multi-lane roads, when passing a streetcar or a vehicle turning left.

    d) On any type of road providing there is an unpaved shoulder.

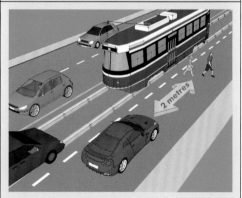

ⓘ When passing a streetcar ensure passengers are not getting on or off. If they are, stay at least 2 m behind the back doors. If a safety island exists, drive cautiously and be on the look-out for pedestrians.

132. Which one of these statements is a basic parking rule?

a) Park on a curve or hill so that you can see ahead.

b) Do not park within 3 m of a fire hydrant.

c) Do not park within 150 m of intersections with traffic lights.

d) Do not look while opening your door.

ⓘ Park where you will not block other parked vehicles, sidewalks or roadways. Never park on a curve, near a crosswalk, fire hydrant or near an intersection. Be careful and watch for cyclists and pedestrians when opening your door.

133. High Occupancy Vehicle lanes on provincial highways are reserved for vehicles carrying at least how many passengers?

a) The driver plus 1 other passenger for a total of 2.

b) The driver plus 2 other passengers for a total of 3.

c) The driver plus 3 other passengers for a total of 4.

d) The driver plus 4 other passengers for a total of 5.

? or More Persons

ⓘ Other roadways will specify the number required. Obey the number of passengers required or risk getting a fine and demerit points. HOV lanes provide many benefits, from reduced traffic to reduced vehicle emissions.

134. What should you do if you hit a deer or moose?

a) Try to move the animal off the road so other vehicles will not hit it.

b) Sound your horn to ward off other animals from coming onto the roadway.

c) Report the incident to the Ministry of Natural Resources or local police.

d) Do nothing but drive cautiously as more animals may be in the area.

ⓘ Never try to move an injured animal as it may increase your chances of being hit by another vehicle.

135. **What should you do if you are the victim of road rage?**

    a) Lock the doors and remain in your vehicle.

    b) If you have a cell phone, safely pull over and call police.

    c) Attract attention to your car by honking the horn and using your signals.

    d) All of the above.

ⓘ Be a polite and courteous driver. Never compete, retaliate or try to educate other drivers, which can lead to road rage.

136. **What should you do when approaching a construction zone?**

    a) Slow down as signs may be posted with reduced speed limits.

    b) Obey all warning signs.

    c) Follow the directions of the traffic control worker.

    d) All of the above.

ⓘ Fines for speeding are doubled when workers are present in construction zones.

137. **What should you do if you feel drowsy while driving?**

    a) Reduce speed.

    b) Turn up your radio.

    c) Take a nap off the road in a safe area.

    d) Open all windows.

ⓘ Drinking coffee or other measures to make you alert are not effective. Driving while drowsy is linked to many accidents so ensure you are well-rested and alert.

138. **Under what circumstances are cell phones not allowed while driving?**
    a) When you use your cell phone to text.
    b) When you use your hand-held cell phone to chat.
    c) When you use your cell phone to check and send emails.
    d) All of the above.

    ⓘ Cell phones distract drivers and can cause accidents. If it is necessary to use a cell phone while driving, only use a hands-free device.

139. **What does the Accessible Parking Permit give you?**
    a) It gives everyone in your family the privilege to park, stand or stop in any area.
    b) Allows parking in designated spaces even if the person with the disability is not a passenger.
    c) Allows parking everywhere during specified times.
    d) Allows parking in designated spaces for you or passengers with you who qualified for the parking permit.

    ⓘ The permit must belong to you or one of your passengers.

140. **When approaching a stopped emergency vehicle with its red lights flashing, you must?…**
    a) Slow down and drive cautiously. You must leave one lane clearance between you and an emergency vehicle if there are multiple lanes in your direction.
    b) Maintain the posted rate of speed for the area.
    c) Slow down, stop and pull over to the right.
    d) Slow down, stop and pull over to the left.

    ⓘ A conviction, fine and demerit points can apply for failing to abide by these rules.

141. How can driver distractions be avoided?

    a) Plan your trip in advance and know where you are going.

    b) Eat before driving to avoid the need to snack.

    c) Preset CD players, radios and other controls before driving.

    d) All of the above.

ⓘ Avoid careless-driving charges and demerit points by avoiding all driving distractions.

---

142. What should you do when glare from bright sunshine makes seeing difficult?

    a) Wear a good pair of sunglasses that cut glare well.

    b) Use your sun visors and adjust them according to the glare.

    c) Reduce speed when entering a tunnel, remove sun glasses, turn on lowbeam headlights.

    d) All of the above.

ⓘ If approaching vehicles at night with glaring headlights, look slightly to the right and above oncoming vehicles. Do not look right at the headlights. Take steps to reduce glare where possible.

---

143. If driving in fog that becomes very dense, what should you do?

    a) Carefully pass vehicles that are moving too slowly or following too closely.

    b) Pull off the road onto the shoulder and wait for the fog to clear.

    c) Turn on emergency flashers and pull off the road completely into a safe parking area.

    d) Slow down and turn on your fog lights.

ⓘ Do not become the first vehicle hit in a chain reaction. Get off the road completely and keep emergency lights flashing. Wait until fog has lifted before driving.

144. **Which statement is false about driving in the rain?**

   a) Rain can reduce visibility.

   b) Rain can fill potholes and cause damage to your car.

   c) Rain can cause your vehicle to hydroplane (ride the water like skis).

   d) Rain can increase your braking ability.

   ⓘ Reduce speed in rain as roads become slippery, especially at the start when moisture mixes with oil and grease from the road surface.

145. **If you skid on a slippery road surface what should you do?**

   a) Steer your vehicle into the direction you want to go.

   b) Steer your vehicle into the opposite direction you want to go.

   c) Apply gas to quickly get out of the skid.

   d) Turn off the ignition.

   ⓘ Skids generally happen because a vehicle is travelling too fast for road, weather or traffic conditions. Always adapt driving accordingly.

146. **What is black ice?**

   a) When snow is mixed with mud and then freezes.

   b) When newly paved roads are wet.

   c) When asphalt has a thin layer of ice on it.

   d) When ice is mixed with snow.

   ⓘ Black ice can form anywhere, especially on bridges which get extra cold air from below. This causes the temperature to drop more quickly on the bridge forming a thin layer of ice.

147. **Snow may be as slippery as ice; what should you do when driving on snow-covered roads?**

    a) Look ahead and slow down.

    b) Avoid steering suddenly.

    c) Avoid braking suddenly.

    d) All of the above.

ⓘ When possible avoid driving in snow by checking weather forecasts regularly. If it is still necessary to drive, do so cautiously.

148. **What should you do if you encounter dangerous whiteout conditions?**

    a) Pass vehicles that are moving too slowly or following too closely.

    b) Pull onto the shoulder and wait for the conditions to change.

    c) Turn on emergency flashers and pull off the road completely into a safe parking area.

    d) Maintain speed and turn on your emergency flashers.

ⓘ Dangerous whiteout conditions can mean serious accidents. Do not risk your life or endanger others. Find a safe parking area and wait for conditions to improve.

149. **What vehicle has flashing blue lights that can be seen 150 m away?**

    a) A school bus.

    b) A tow truck.

    c) A snow removal vehicle.

    d) An ambulance.

ⓘ Snow removal vehicles are slow and can be wide. To clear highways there may be groups of them across the road. Do not try to speed around them.

150. **If driving and your brakes fail what should you do?**
    a) Turn off the ignition.
    b) Keep your foot on the brake and apply strong downward pressure.
    c) Pump the brakes to restore hydraulic brake pressure.
    d) Sound horn and steer to a clear area.

    ⓘ Regular vehicle service with brake checking is the best way to avoid brake failure.

151. **What should you do if your gas pedal sticks?**
    a) First try to lift the pedal with your foot.
    b) First try to reach down and lift the pedal with your hands.
    c) Sound your horn to warn others of your problem.
    d) Drive onto a sidewalk.

    ⓘ If lifting the pedal with your foot does not work, turn on your emergency lights, shift into neutral and gradually stop, ideally off the road.

152. **What should you do if your car is about to stall on the highway?**
    a) Honk your horn for help.
    b) Stop and put on your hazard lights.
    c) Pull over to the closest shoulder as quickly as possible.
    d) Continue at a reduced speed; you may not even have a problem.

    ⓘ Pull over to the shoulder as carefully and quickly as possible by slowing down, checking all mirrors and putting on your emergency lights.

153. What should you do if you have a tire blow-out?

a) Step on the gas pedal and quickly move off the road.

b) Firmly steer into the safest direction and remove your foot from the gas pedal.

c) Stop and put on your hazard lights.

d) Honk your horn for help.

ⓘ Blow-outs at high speeds can be very dangerous. Remain calm, take your foot off the gas pedal and firmly steer where you want to go.

154. If you are in an accident with no personal injuries and damages are less $1,000, you should?...

a) Call 911 even if damages are less than $1,000.

b) Move driveable vehicles off the road to enable traffic to move freely, and exchange information.

c) Leave cars with damages where they are so that police can determine fault.

d) Call an ambulance in case someone hits your car and gets hurt.

ⓘ As long as no one is hurt and damages are less than $1000, move driveable vehicles off the road safely to allow traffic to flow. Then call police services, not 911, and obtain the closest Collision Reporting Centre to report the accident.

155. If you are in an accident with no personal injuries, but damages are over $1,000, you should?

a) Exchange information with the other party and leave.

b) Call police and give them information about the accident and damages.

c) Leave the scene, as "no fault" insurance handles this.

d) All of the above.

ⓘ Provide as much information to police about the accident as possible giving them information about vehicles and damages. Also obtain witness contact information to give police.

156. When involved in or witness to an accident where someone has been injured, you should?...

a) Call or have someone else call for help immediately.

b) Turn off the vehicle and turn on the emergency lights.

c) If you are not injured, stay calm and offer help until emergency services arrive.

d) All of the above.

ⓘ In case of a fuel leak ensure no one is smoking or lights a match. Call for help. Stay calm and cover accident victims with a blanket or jacket to reduce shock.

157. If a police officer or inspector from the MTO deems your vehicle unsafe, what can happen?

a) Your vehicle can be taken off the road.

b) Your licence plates can be removed and taken.

c) You could be fined up to $1,000 if you refuse the inspection.

d) All of the above.

ⓘ You must fix whatever problem is identified during an inspection by a police officer or inspector from the Ontario Ministry of Transportation (MTO) before you can put your vehicle safely and legally back on the road.

158. When and how often do you have to renew your driver's licence?

a) Whenever you receive a renewal application in the mail.

b) You do not have to renew as you have already passed all required tests.

c) Every 10 years.

d) Every 20 years.

ⓘ If you do not receive a renewal application or renewal postcard in the mail you are still responsible for ensuring you have a valid driver's licence that has not expired. Contact the Ministry of Transportation for further information.

159. **If there are continuity lines to the right of your vehicle in the lane you are in what must you do?**

    a) You must turn into another lane as your lane is exiting or ending.

    b) You are not required to do anything unless you want to exit. Your lane is unaffected.

    c) You must merge with the traffic to your left.

    d) You must merge with the traffic to your right.

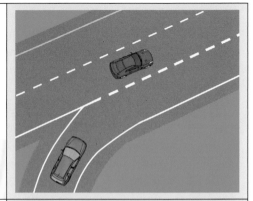

ⓘ White lines closer together and wider than other white lines are continuity lines. Continuity lines to your left mean your lane is ending so you must turn or exit. Continuity lines to your right mean your lane is unaffected.

160. **On a vehicle's left side what does a broken yellow pavement marking beside a solid yellow line mean?**

    a) Cars travelling in the other direction may pass when the way is clear.

    b) You may pass when the way is clear.

    c) No cars may pass in either direction.

    d) Both cars may pass in either direction when the way is clear.

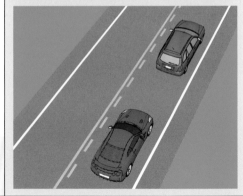

ⓘ Broken yellow lines in the lane to your left mean you may pass when the way is clear. There may even be a solid yellow line to the left of that, meaning you may still pass when clear but vehicles in the opposite direction may not.

161. If a traffic light is red, but there is a green arrow pointing left, what does that mean?

a) Vehicles in the left turning lane may turn left.

b) Vehicles in the left turning lane may turn right.

c) No vehicles may turn—only pedestrians may cross.

d) The direction of the green arrow indicates there is a one-way street.

ⓘ Vehicles in both directions may be turning left. If the arrow turns yellow, a green light will soon appear in one or more directions. Stop if you can safely; if not, complete a left turn cautiously.

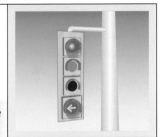

162. What does the round signal with a white vertical line on it represent in the picture?

a) It is a left turn signal.

b) It is a spare light should the other ones malfunction.

c) It is a symbol indicating pedestrians may not cross.

d) It is a transit priority signal allowing public transit vehicles the right-of-way.

ⓘ Pedestrians and non-public transit vehicles must stop on the red light and yield the right-of-way to transit vehicles.

163. Some left turn lanes have their own traffic light to direct traffic. What does this light mean?

a) Pedestrians crossing the street towards the left may cross.

b) All traffic facing the traffic light may turn left or proceed straight.

c) Vehicles in the left turn lane may turn left while other vehicles will face a red light.

d) This is a transit priority signal.

ⓘ When you see this signal and you are turning left you may face other vehicles from the opposite direction also making left turns.

164. What does a flashing amber or yellow light mean?

a) Slow down and drive with caution.

b) Stop and proceed when it is safe.

c) Stop and turn left.

d) Stop and turn right.

ⓘ Flashing amber lights whether alone or within a traffic light warn you to slow down and proceed cautiously in the direction you are going.

165. What does a flashing red traffic light mean?

a) Slow down and drive with caution.

b) Stop and proceed when it is safe.

c) Stop and turn left.

d) Stop and turn right.

ⓘ Always bring your vehicle to a complete stop. Proceed into the intersection only when it is safe to do so.

166. What does an amber or yellow light mean?

a) Speed up and clear the intersection so you do not block traffic when the light changes.

b) Proceed with caution only if you cannot stop in time.

c) Keep going and do not stop as another car can hit you from behind.

d) There is road construction ahead so slow down and proceed with caution.

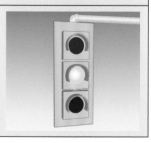

ⓘ If you can stop safely you must do so; otherwise proceed with caution. The light will be turning red soon, at which point you should be stopped.

167. Which statement is correct regarding red lights?

    a) You may turn right on a red light, unless otherwise posted, provided you stop first.

    b) From a one-way street to a one-way street you may turn left after slowing for a red light.

    c) If you are in a hurry you may drive through red lights with caution only if the way is clear.

    d) All of the above.

  🛈 You must always come to a complete stop at the appropriate road markings or intersection edge on a red light before making any turns.

168. What do advanced green lights tell you?

    a) You have the right-of-way to go in any direction in the intersection from the correct lane.

    b) They allow pedestrians to go first.

    c) A flashing green light means only vehicles turning left may do so.

    d) None of the above.

  🛈 When facing an advanced green light, oncoming traffic faces a red light, enabling you to turn left, go straight or turn right from the appropriate lane.

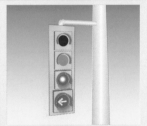

169. If pedestrians face a walk signal, what should they do?

    a) Cross the road in the direction of the symbol with the right-of-way over vehicles.

    b) Cross the road in the direction of the symbol yielding the right-of-way to vehicles.

    c) Stop and yield the right-of-way to vehicles.

    d) Cross the intersection in any direction.

  🛈 Vehicles must always be aware of their surroundings and yield the right-of-way to pedestrians crossing or those who need more time to cross.

170. **What do the white markings in this diagram represent?**
    a) Two parallel white lines at an intersection indicate a crosswalk for pedestrians.
    b) They indicate there is a one-way street to the right.
    c) These solid lines indicate there is no passing in either direction.
    d) These do not indicate anything different from the other directions.

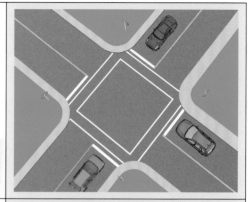

ⓘ Intersections may have a stop line, parallel lines or a sidewalk. If these are absent, stop at the intersection edge in order to allow pedestrians to cross; and remember, no passing within 30 m of a crosswalk.

171. **What is the best way to check your blind spots?**
    a) Through your side mirrors.
    b) Through your rear view mirrors.
    c) Turning your head and doing shoulder checks.
    d) Asking your passengers to check for you.

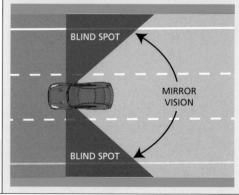

ⓘ Mirrors can help reduce the extent of blind spots but they will not get rid of them entirely; only shoulder checks will. Adjust all mirrors to minimize blind spots.

172. How long must new drivers hold a Class G1 licence before their G1 Road Test?

a) 6 months.

b) 12 months.

c) 18 months.

d) 2 years.

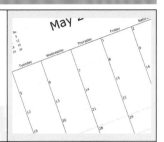

ⓘ If you take a Ministry approved Beginner Driver Education Course while you have your G1 licence and pass it, you can apply for your G1 road test in 8 months.

173. What level must your blood alcohol level be if you hold a Class G1 licence?

a) Less than 1.0.

b) Less than .08.

c) Less than .05.

d) 0.

ⓘ You must have a blood alcohol level of 0; therefore, no alcohol. If you are caught drinking and driving you will get a licence suspension. You will also face penalties that are becoming tougher.

174. How many passengers may you have in a vehicle if you have a Class G1 licence?

a) Only the other driver with a Class G licence may be in the backseat of the car.

b) Up to a maximum of 4.

c) As many as there are working seatbelts.

d) No other passengers may be in the car with you.

ⓘ Passengers must not exceed the amount of working seatbelts. Included must be a Class G driver, meeting all requirements, in the front passenger seat.

175. What are the requirements of the G Class driver that may accompany a G1 driver?

a) The G Class driver must be in the front passenger seat.

b) The G Class driver must have at least 4 years of driving experience.

c) The G Class driver must have less than a .05 % blood alcohol level; 0% if under 22 years old.

d) All of the above.

ⓘ Included in the G Class driver's experience is any valid G2 level experience.

176. What are you not allowed to do when you have your G1 licence?

a) Drive on roads with speeds greater than 100 km/h; drive between midnight and 5:00 a.m.

b) Drive on roads with speeds greater than 80 km/h; drive between midnight and 5:00 a.m.

c) Drive on roads with speeds greater than 80 km/h; drive between 9:00 p.m. and 6:00 a.m.

d) Drive on roads with speeds greater than 100 km/h; drive between 9:00 p.m. and 6:00 a.m.

ⓘ There are also certain highways you may not drive on. Consult the Ministry of Transportation if unsure which 400-series highways or other highways a G1 driver may drive on.

177. Which of the following is false about Level 2 (Class G2) drivers?

a) You may drive between midnight and 5:00 a.m.

b) You may have a blood alcohol level of .05 or less.

c) Depending on your age and if no G Class driver is with you, there may be passenger restrictions between midnight and 5:00 a.m.

d) Each passenger must have a working seatbelt.

ⓘ Since G2 lasts at least 12 months, more privileges exist with this class than with G1 drivers. However, alcohol is not one of them. If in doubt about Class G2 privileges see page 6 and also consult the Ministry of Transportation.

178. What changes must you tell the Ministry of Transportation about?

a) If your name has changed.

b) If your address has changed.

c) If you have a different vehicle such as a new car.

d) All of the above.

ⓘ When your name, address or any major physical change to your car occurs, you must tell the Ministry of Transportation within six days.

179. Which of these statements is not true?

a) You may not use a licence which has been altered.

b) You may not use an imitation licence.

c) You are allowed to have more than one Ontario licence.

d) You may not lend your licence to anyone or let anyone borrow it.

ⓘ There are licence laws that all licensed drivers must follow, or face a fine.

180. Which of these situations may result in a driving suspension after a court order?

a) If you have a medical condition that affects your ability to drive.

b) If you do not have your vehicle properly insured.

c) If you drive over the speed limit by 50 km/h or greater.

d) All of the above.

ⓘ You need to abide by all safety measures affecting you, others and your vehicle. Driving while under suspension will result in hefty fines, possible jail time and vehicle impoundment.

181. If you refuse a police roadside blood alcohol screening test what can happen?

a) You get a warning that will go on your record and you cannot refuse when asked next time.

b) You have 24 hours to show up for a test.

c) You have the option of going to the police station and taking a breathalyzer test.

d) Your licence will be suspended and you can face criminal charges.

(i) You must participate in a screening test. Do not avoid it by thinking you can "get off" the charges. Instead you will be charged with failing to provide a breath sample and the conviction is the same as for impaired driving.

182. What can give you a suspension or impaired driving charge?

a) If you hold a G1 or G2 licence and your blood alcohol level is over 0.

b) If you have a blood alcohol level over .05.

c) If you are behind the wheel of a turned-off vehicle, but your blood alcohol level is over .08.

d) All of the above.

(i) Having a blood alcohol content from .05–.08, known as the "warn range", will now give you a licence suspension which will increase with each occurrence. Your age and blood alcohol content also impacts suspension time.

183. What does compulsory automobile insurance mean?

a) You must have a valid driver's licence to drive on roads.

b) Any passenger must have a valid driver's licence.

c) You must have insurance coverage.

d) Any passengers with you must have insurance coverage.

(i) The Compulsory Automobile Insurance Act (CAIA) requires all Ontario drivers to carry proof that they are insured. You also have to insure all your vehicles with third party liability insurance of at least $200,000.

184. **If you change the colour of your vehicle, what are you required to do?**

   a) Tell the Driver and Vehicle Licence Issuing Office within 6 days of the change.

   b) Tell the Driver and Vehicle Licence Issuing Office within 60 days of the change.

   c) Nothing, just ensure your vehicle meets safety standards.

   d) Book an emissions test with Drive Clean.

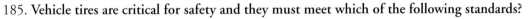 Your vehicle registration has 2 parts, licence plate and vehicle permit. The vehicle permit must have an accurate description of your vehicle, so any changes must be reported.

185. **Vehicle tires are critical for safety and they must meet which of the following standards?**

   a) Have a minimum tread of 1.5 mm.

   b) Not have any knots, exposed cords, bumps, bulges, etc., making them unsafe.

   c) Match on all 4 wheels as some combinations are illegal.

   d) All of the above.

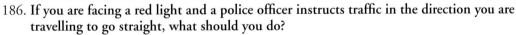 Check your owners manual for tire safety tips as each will vary depending on vehicle make and weight.

186. **If you are facing a red light and a police officer instructs traffic in the direction you are travelling to go straight, what should you do?**

   a) First stop at the intersection and then proceed.

   b) Slow down to 40 km/h and then proceed through.

   c) Follow the direction of the police officer despite what the traffic light or road sign indicates.

   d) Treat the intersection as a four-way stop.

ⓘ Always follow the direction of a police officer that is directing traffic.

187. **If towing a trailer that is 2.05 m wide or less, what must it have?**
   a) Two far-apart red reflectors at the back, a white licence plate light and a red tail light.
   b) Flashing yellow lights at the rear.
   c) Flashing red lights at the rear.
   d) None of the above.

ⓘ Ensure your trailer has the proper lights and reflectors. Requirements vary depending on trailer width. Never carry passengers in a moving trailer.

188. **Can anyone tow a trailer with a gross weight of up to 4600 kg?**
   a) As long as you have a valid G, G1, G2 or higher driver's licence.
   b) As long as you have a valid G, G1, G2 or higher driver's licence plus a trailer plate and permit.
   c) As long as your trailer has trailer plates.
   d) Only if you have your commercial vehicle licence.

ⓘ A trailer requires a special permit and plates that you need to obtain, and a one-time charge, from a Vehicle Licence Issuing Office.

189. **Which of the below infractions may cause you to receive 2 demerit points?**
    a) Failure to stop for a police officer.
    b) Reckless or careless driving.
    c) Exceeding posted speed limits by more than 50 km/h.
    d) Having passengers under 16 not wearing their seatbelts.

ⓘ Many infractions exist where you may receive a fine and/or 2 demerit points. Infraction "a" will give you 7 demerit points, while "b" and "c" will give you 6. Demerit points on your record stay for 2 years from the offence date.

190. **What if you are a G1 or G2 driver and you have 9 or more demerit points within 2 years?**
    a) You must surrender your licence—your licence will be suspended for 6 days.
    b) You must surrender your licence—your licence will be suspended for 60 days.
    c) You must surrender your licence—your licence will be suspended for 120 days.
    d) You will receive a warning letter in the mail to improve your driving.

ⓘ If you fail to surrender your licence to the Ministry of Transportation, you may lose your licence for up to 2 years. After suspension your demerit point total will be 4. Any other infractions you get will be added to this.

191. **The G2 road test includes highway driving, but before the test, what must you do?**
    a) Show the instructor your G1 licence.
    b) Rewrite your G1 level test and get a higher score than on your first test.
    c) Sign a "Declaration of Highway Driving Experience" detailing your highway driving history.
    d) Pass a colour blindness test.

ⓘ Among other details on the declaration form, you must indicate how many times in the last 3 months you drove on a highway, which highways and for how much time.

192. What does this hand signal mean?

    a) Driver in vehicle is slowing down or stopping.

    b) Driver in vehicle is turning right.

    c) Driver in vehicle is turning left.

    d) Driver in vehicle is exiting a highway.

ℹ If your brake lights or turn signals do not work, ensure you use proper hand signals to warn other drivers of your intentions. Use both for clarity if in doubt.

193. What does this hand signal mean?

    a) Driver in vehicle is slowing down or stopping.

    b) Driver in vehicle is turning right.

    c) Driver in vehicle is turning left.

    d) Driver in vehicle is exiting a highway.

ℹ If your brake lights or turn signals do not work, ensure you use proper hand signals to warn other drivers of your intentions. Use both for clarity if in doubt.

194. What does this hand signal mean?

    a) Driver in vehicle is slowing down or stopping.

    b) Driver in vehicle is turning right.

    c) Driver in vehicle is turning left.

    d) Driver in vehicle is exiting a highway.

ℹ If your brake lights or turn signals do not work, ensure you use proper hand signals to warn other drivers of your intentions. Use both for clarity if in doubt.

195. As a buyer of a privately used vehicle what must you get from the seller?

    a) The seller's licence plates and permit.

    b) The seller's driver's licence.

    c) A bill of sale.

    d) A Used Vehicle Information Package.

ⓘ The package will include details about the vehicle for the buyer's benefit. The new owner of a used vehicle has to register their new vehicle within 6 days at a Driver and Vehicle Licence Issuing Office with required documents.

196. How many days do new Ontario residents have to register their vehicles?

    a) 30 days.

    b) 60 days.

    c) 90 days.

    d) 120 days.

ⓘ A vehicle permit and licence plate can be obtained at a Driver and Vehicle Licence Issuing Office. Bring all required information.

197. What does vehicle registration include?

    a) Licence plates and a vehicle permit.

    b) Obtaining your G1 licence.

    c) Obtaining your G2 licence.

    d) None of the above.

ⓘ In Ontario, licence plates do not move with vehicles, they move with vehicle owners. When you buy a new car your existing plates go with you. All vehicle changes must be reported to a Driver and Vehicle Licence Issuing Office.

198. What should you do when entering a freeway?

    a) Signal, then stop to wait for an opening in traffic.

    b) Signal, then accelerate while merging smoothly into traffic.

    c) Signal, then accelerate and enter traffic quickly.

    d) Do what the vehicle ahead of you does.

ⓘ Be sure to check your mirrors and blind spots as you move along the entrance ramp.

199. What should you do when exiting a freeway?

    a) Signal, then stop to wait for an opening in traffic.

    b) Signal, accelerate while merging smoothly into traffic, then proceed to the exit lane.

    c) Signal, move into the deceleration lane, reduce speed gradually and obey exit signs.

    d) Do what the vehicle ahead of you does.

ⓘ Ensure you slow down enough when in the deceleration lane because you may not realize how fast you are going, having come off the freeway at a higher speed.

200. **What does the term "overdriving your headlights" mean?**

   a) You are leaving your lowbeam lights on too long at the risk of burning out the bulbs.

   b) You are leaving your highbeam headlights on too long at the risk of burning out the bulbs.

   c) You are driving slower than your stopping distance allows you to see.

   d) You are driving faster than your stopping distance allows you to see.

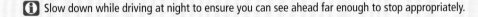 Slow down while driving at night to ensure you can see ahead far enough to stop appropriately.

201. **What should you do when you hear bells or sirens or see flashing lights?**

   a) Slow down, move to the far right of the roadway and stop when it is safe to do so. Do not block the shoulder if on a freeway.

   b) Slow down and move to the far left of the roadway but do not stop.

   c) Come to a complete stop wherever you are.

   d) Speed up and keep the movement of traffic going.

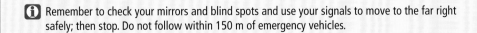 Remember to check your mirrors and blind spots and use your signals to move to the far right safely; then stop. Do not follow within 150 m of emergency vehicles.

202. When sitting on a motorcycle seat how far from the ground should your feet be?

a) Only your toes should be able to touch the ground.

b) Your toes should be 5–10 cm (2–4 inches) from the ground.

c) Your feet should rest flat 2.54 cm (1 inch) from the ground.

d) Your feet should rest flat on the ground.

ℹ️ Make sure your motorcycle is safe and comfortable. Start by ensuring your feet rest flat on the ground when sitting on the seat. If they do not the motorcycle may be too big for you.

203. What must you ensure if you carry passengers?

a) Your passenger must wear an approved helmet.

b) Your motorcycle must carry footrests for the passenger.

c) Your seat must be large enough to carry you and a passenger comfortably.

d) All of the above.

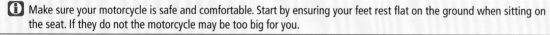

ℹ️ Additionally you must have more than your M1 licence as it is illegal to carry passengers with only your M1. Even M2 licence holders are encouraged not to carry passengers until they are more experienced.

204. Besides headlights and tail lights on your motorcycle, what else makes you visible at night?

a) Wearing brown, navy, black or other dark clothing with a dark helmet.

b) Wearing orange, yellow, red or other bright clothing with a bright helmet.

c) Wearing a reflective vest or having reflective stripes in your jacket.

d) Both b and c.

ℹ️ Most motorcycle accidents are due to the motorcyclist not being seen by other drivers. Wearing brightly coloured gear is one of the best ways to make yourself more visible.

205. Why do you need a Safety Standards Certificate if you are buying a used motorcycle?

a) You cannot drive or put your plates on a vehicle without it.

b) It may be the 5-year mark where all vehicles must pass a safety check.

c) All of the above.

d) None of the above.

ⓘ The Ministry of Transportation licenses inspection stations to inspect and certify motorcycles. You must obtain this certificate to prove your motorcycle passed inspection. After the inspection, the certificate is valid for 36 days.

206. The Highway Traffic Act categorizes which of these groups as a motorcycle?

a) Motor tricycles, limited speed motorcycles, and mopeds.

b) Motor tricycles and limited speed motorcycles.

c) Motor tricycles and mopeds.

d) Limited speed motorcycles and mopeds.

ⓘ The Highway Traffic Act does not consider mopeds as motorcycles, but to drive a moped legally on roads, you have to register it and have valid plates.

207. To legally drive a motorcycle on the road, you must?…

a) Be 16 years old or older.

b) Have a valid M1, M2, or M licence.

c) Have a valid licence plate attached to the rear of your motorcycle.

d) All of the above.

ⓘ A helmet is also required. Additionally you must register your motorcycle and have the required liability insurance.

208. Is it necessary to have a horn on your motorcycle?

    a) Not only is it necessary, the horn must work.

    b) A horn is only necessary for mopeds.

    c) Horns are not necessary on motorcycles.

    d) None of the above.

ⓘ Both motorcycles and mopeds must have a functioning horn. This is for the rider's safety.

209. Which statement is FALSE regarding M1 licence conditions?

    a) Only drive during daylight hours from 1/2 an hour before sunrise to 1/2 an hour after sunset.

    b) Your blood alcohol level must be under .05

    c) You must not have any passengers.

    d) You must not drive on certain roads or exceed a certain speed.

ⓘ You must not drive if you have consumed any alcohol. Your blood alcohol level must be 0.

210. When can you take the Level 1 road test in order to get your M2 licence?

    a) After having your M1 licence for 30 days.

    b) After having your M1 licence for 60 days.

    c) After having your M1 licence for 90 days.

    d) After having your M1 licence for 120 days.

ⓘ You must also take your road test before your M1 licence expires, which is 90 days from date of issue. If enrolled in a Ministry-approved rider training course, you may take the M1 Exit test at any time, but Ministry timelines still apply for registering it.

211. **If you pass the Level 1 road test using a limited-speed motorcycle which licence will you get?**

a) An M2 licence.

b) An M2 licence with an M condition.

c) An M2 licence with an L condition.

d) An M2 licence with both an L and M condition.

ⓘ Type of vehicle will determine the type of licence you will receive. Using a moped or limited-speed motorcycle and passing the Level 1 road test will result in an M2 licence with an L condition.

212. **What do you need to bring to the Level 1 road test toward your M2 licence?**

a) A vehicle in good working order meeting Ministry standards for the licence class tested on.

b) A motorcycle helmet that meets regulations set out by the Highway Traffic Act.

c) Corrective eyewear if required for driving, such as glasses or contacts.

d) All of the above.

ⓘ Additionally you will be required to bring your M1 licence to the Level 1 road test.

213. **Which statement is FALSE regarding M2 licence conditions?**

a) You can drive anytime, day or night.

b) Your blood alcohol level must be under .05.

c) You may carry passengers (mopeds excluded).

d) None of the above.

ⓘ At the M2 level you have fewer restrictions than you do at the M1 level; however, alcohol is still one of them. You must maintain a blood alcohol level of 0 at all times when driving at this level.

214. Where is the front brake located and how do you apply it?

a) It is on the right handlebar and it is applied by pulling the lever toward the handgrip.

b) It is on the left handlebar and it is applied by pulling the lever toward the handgrip.

c) It is on the right handlebar and it is applied by pushing the lever away from the handgrip.

d) It is on the left handlebar and it is applied by pushing the lever away from the handgrip.

ⓘ Front and rear brakes should be used together at all times even though the front brake provides more stopping power.

215. Which of the following is not a primary control that is important for motorcycle operation?

a) Shift lever.

b) Rear brake

c) Throttle.

d) Speedometer.

ⓘ While all controls are important, primary ones are listed from a–c and include handlebars, front brake and clutch.

216. What function does the throttle perform?

a) It controls the motorcycle's gears.

b) It controls the motorcycle's rear brakes.

c) It controls the motorcycle's speed in conjunction with the clutch.

d) It shows the revolutions the engine is turning per minute.

ⓘ A motorcycle's speed is controlled by the throttle which is on the right handgrip. Fuel flows to the engine when the throttle is twisted toward you. This is in conjunction with releasing the clutch located on the left handgrip.

217. **How often should you check your motorcycle tires for proper tread, pressure or damage?**
   a) Every year.
   b) Every month.
   c) Every week.
   d) Every time you get on a motorcycle.

   ℹ️ You are more susceptible to danger should something go wrong with your motorcycle. Tires, brakes, controls, lights, and cables are just some of the things you should check every time you get on a motorcycle.

218. **Why is it important to adjust your mirrors?**
   a) So that you can see at least half the lane behind you.
   b) So that you can see most of the lane beside you.
   c) So that you can reduce your blind spot.
   d) All of the above.

   ℹ️ Properly adjusted mirrors help you see what is around you and they should also be used with shoulder checks. Checking mirrors should not replace a shoulder check.

219. **How often should you check your mirrors while driving?**
   a) Every 2–4 seconds.
   b) Every 5–7 seconds.
   c) Every 8–10 seconds.
   d) Every 11–13 seconds.

   ℹ️ Avoid surprises, especially before turning, changing lanes or slowing down, by checking your mirrors every 5–7 seconds. Check more frequently on highways or when conditions are not ideal.

220. What is the best way to learn how to safely drive a motorcycle?

a) From a friend who drives a motorcycle.

b) From reading a lot of motorcycle driving material.

c) By taking a motorcycle safety course that is approved by the Ministry.

d) None of the above.

ⓘ A Ministry-approved motorcycle safety course will teach you required skills and knowledge. Most branches include the first road test as part of the course fee and courses enable you to shorten time spent at Level 2 by 4 months.

221. If your motorcycle headlights do not turn on automatically, when must you have them on?

a) Whenever it rains.

b) At all times, day or night.

c) Whenever conditions require you to turn them on.

d) From ½ an hour before sunset to ½ an hour after sunrise.

ⓘ It is advisable to have both headlights and tail lights on at all times. With most motorcycles they automatically turn on when the vehicle is started. Older motorcycles with switches need to be turned on at the required times.

222. What is counter-steering or push-steering?

a) Counting the appropriate number of seconds in order to complete a turn accurately.

b) Putting forward pressure on the handlebar on the turning side (right handlebar for right turn).

c) A process that involves your motorcycle and you leaning in the direction you want to turn.

d) Both b and c.

ⓘ Putting forward pressure on a handlebar causes you and your motorcycle to lean. Push on the opposite handlebar and add throttle to straighten and to complete the turn. This is called counter-steering or push-steering.

223. What is the best way to see everything around you?

    a) Look far enough ahead: 1/2 a block to a block ahead in the city, further on freeways.

    b) Constantly scan the road in all directions by not looking in one place for more than 2 seconds.

    c) Look at side streets and curbs ensuring vehicles entering see you and you see them.

    d) All of the above.

ⓘ Maximize your visibility to avoid sudden surprises which can catch you off guard and result a collision.

224. What is the best way to be seen at intersections?

    a) Speed up when approaching intersections so other drivers can see you before they proceed.

    b) Move closer to other vehicles so that they can see you better.

    c) Slow down when approaching intersections and move away from cars or things blocking you.

    d) None of the above.

ⓘ Avoid collisions at intersections, which commonly involve motorcyclists, by keeping you and your motorcycle in view of others. Also, approach intersections slowly.

225. How can you communicate with other drivers?

    a) Use signals and flash your brake lights.

    b) Use signals, flash your brake lights and make eye contact with other drivers.

    c) Use signals, flash your brake lights and perform shoulder checks.

    d) Use signals, flash your brake lights, make eye contact with other drivers, perform shoulder checks and sound your horn if required.

ⓘ The more you communicate with other drivers the more your safety will be ensured because you will be seen.

226. **What should you do when you are being passed by an oncoming vehicle or from behind?**

a) Move toward the right tire track.

b) Move toward the left tire track.

c) Move toward the centre part of the lane.

d) Stay in the lane position you are in.

ⓘ Position yourself to be a safe distance from any passing vehicle by moving toward the centre of the lane.

227. **What dangers do large vehicles pose to motorcycle drivers?**

a) They have small blindspots.

b) They make wide turns.

c) They may roll forward after stopping.

d) They block large amounts of snow and slush from your vehicle.

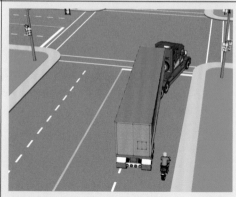

ⓘ Always leave enough space around large vehicles by staying well back. Large vehicles make wide turns so do not move into any open space if they are turning as you may be squeezed between the curb and the large vehicle.

228. What must you remember to do first whenever you change gears?

a) You must disengage the throttle.

b) You must disengage the clutch.

c) You must disengage the tachometer.

d) You must engage the engine kill switch.

(i) The lever located on the left handlebar is the clutch and when it is squeezed toward you it is disengaged. You must do this before changing gears in conjunction with releasing the throttle.

229. How long does it take to get your full M licence?

a) 60 days.

b) 90 days.

c) 12 months.

d) 20 months.

(i) Obtaining your M licence is a graduated process, just like getting your G licence, taking a minimum of 20 months.

230. How much distance should you keep between you and other drivers?

a) At least a 2-second distance.

b) At least a 12-second distance.

c) At least a 1-second distance.

d) At least a 10-second distance.

(i) Driving a minimum 2-second distance behind any vehicle allows you to see well enough ahead to prepare for any upcoming hazards and react to them.

231. Why is it important to slow down when driving at night behind other vehicles?

    a) So the distance between you and vehicles in front is lessened and so other drivers can see you.

    b) So the distance between you and vehicles in front is greater and so other drivers can see you.

    c) So the distance between you and the vehicle in front is the same.

    d) None of the above.

ⓘ Ensure your safety and allow yourself to be seen especially if roads are wet and when excessive glare can cause other drivers to not see your single motorcycle light among other vehicle lights.

232. What does this hand signal mean?

    a) Driver on motorcycle is slowing down or stopping.

    b) Driver on motorcycle is turning right.

    c) Driver on motorcycle is turning left.

    d) Driver in vehicle is exiting a highway.

ⓘ If your motorcycle does not have turn signals, use proper hand signals to warn others of your intentions.

233. What does this hand signal mean?

    a) Driver on motorcycle is slowing down or stopping.

    b) Driver on motorcycle is turning right.

    c) Driver on motorcycle is turning left.

    d) Driver in vehicle is exiting a highway.

ⓘ If your motorcycle does not have turn signals, use proper hand signals to warn others of your intentions.

234. **After coming out of a parked position at the side of the road, which way should you position your motorcycle?**

    a) Position your motorcycle in the direction you want to go.

    b) Position your motorcycle in the opposite direction you want to go.

    c) Angle your motorcycle across the roadway so that you can clearly see in both directions.

    d) None of the above.

ⓘ Especially if there are cars on either side of you, angle your motorcycle so that you can be seen and so that you can see in both directions.

235. **What should you remember about blind spots?**

    a) Do not drive in someone else's blind spot.

    b) Do not let another vehicle drive in your blind spot.

    c) None of the above.

    d) Both a and b.

ⓘ Lane position is extremely important so change it often in order to reduce your blind spot and also to avoid driving in another vehicle's blind spot.

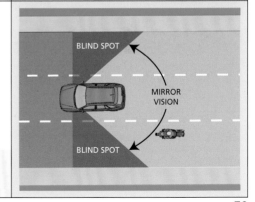

79

236. What does this hand signal mean?

a) Driver on motorcycle is slowing down or stopping.

b) Driver on motorcycle is turning right.

c) Driver on motorcycle is turning left.

d) Driver in vehicle is exiting a highway.

ℹ If your motorcycle does not have turn signals, use proper hand signals to warn others of your intentions.

237. Which is not a tip for driving in the rain?

a) Make all moves smoothly, avoiding sudden moves which can cause a skid.

b) Drive in the appropriate lane position to avoid oil, grease, and debris on the roadway.

c) Wear reflective and bright clothing so you can easily be seen.

d) Use only the front brake to ensure you stop in time.

ℹ Always use both brakes to stop, especially when the road is slippery.

238. What is lane splitting?

a) When a car and a motorcycle share a lane.

b) When two motorcyclists share a lane.

c) When you drive a motorcycle between lanes on the marked white lines.

d) All of the above.

ℹ Never attempt lane splitting as other vehicles will not expect you to be there and may not see you, resulting in a possible collision.

239. **Why is it important to leave a cushion of space around you?**
   a) So that you can react to a difficult situation in time.
   b) So that you can avoid a difficult situation and move to another place in time.
   c) So that you can clearly be seen by other drivers which maximizes your protection against a collision.
   d) All of the above.

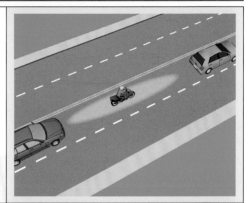

ⓘ The greater distance you have between you and other drivers, the greater protection you have from a collision.

240. **How can turbulence from large vehicles dangerously affect motorcyclists?**
   a) Excessive airflow can threaten your ability to control your motorcycle when you pass.
   b) Excessive air pressure can threaten your ability to control your motorcycle when you pass.
   c) Both a and b.
   d) None of the above.

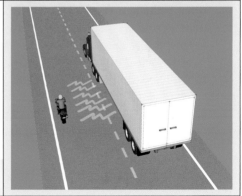

ⓘ Be extra cautious when passing large vehicles and learn the fundamentals of passing them, especially at high speeds where turbulence is greatest.

241. Why is lane or blocking position important and where is it best to be?

a) Lane position is important for protection and it is best to drive in the centre of the lane.

b) Lane position is important for protection and it is best to only drive in the right tire track.

c) Lane position is important for protection and it is best to only drive in the left tire track.

d) Lane position is important for protection and it is best to drive in the appropriate tire track for the road conditions or traffic.

ⓘ To ensure your protection you must be seen. To be seen you need to select an appropriate lane position, either right or left tire track depending on road conditions and traffic.

242. What is the best way to ensure your safety when vehicles are turning left in front of you?

a) Slow down, check all around you, move to the right of your lane, have a plan of action if a vehicle turns directly in front of you.

b) Slow down, check all around you, move to the left of your lane, have a plan of action if a vehicle turns directly in front of you.

c) Maintain speed, check all around you, move to the right of your lane, have a plan of action if a vehicle turns directly in front of you.

d) None of the above.

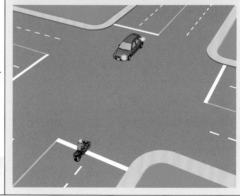

ⓘ Most accidents between cars and motorcycles occur at intersections because cars turning left can not see a motorcycle or they misjudge how fast it is travelling. So use extra caution.

243. **Why is overdriving your headlights dangerous?**
   a) You will not have enough distance to stop safely.
   b) You are travelling faster than your headlights allow you to see.
   c) None of the above.
   d) Both a and b.

ℹ️ Slow down while driving at night to ensure you can see far enough ahead to stop appropriately.

244. **What blocking position or tire track should you be in if turning right in a wide lane?**
   a) In the left tire track.
   b) In the right tire track.
   c) In the centre tire track.
   d) It doesn't matter as long as you feel comfortable.

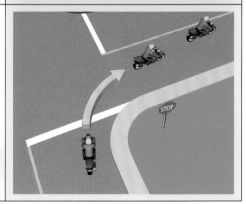

ℹ️ Block your lane in the direction of the turn. In a wide lane the stop line is further out requiring you to move to the right tire track to avoid another vehicle coming up beside you. It is even advisable to angle your bike because you are more visible on an angle.

245. **If a bus is coming out of a bus bay and you are behind it, who has the right-of-way?**

    a) You have the right-of-way.

    b) The bus has the right-of-way.

    c) Whoever got there first has the right-of-way.

    d) Traffic in the intersection has the right-of-way.

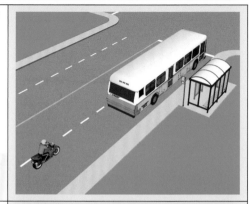

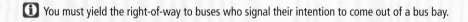 You must yield the right-of-way to buses who signal their intention to come out of a bus bay.

246. **What tire track position should you be in if turning left from a curb lane into a curb lane?**

    a) In the left tire track.

    b) In the right tire track.

    c) In the centre tire track.

    d) It doesn't matter as long as you feel comfortable.

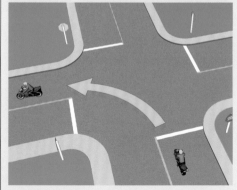

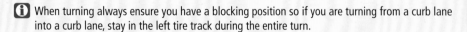 When turning always ensure you have a blocking position so if you are turning from a curb lane into a curb lane, stay in the left tire track during the entire turn.

247. **When can a motorcycle pass on a shoulder?**
    a) Only if a vehicle is turning left and you have an unpaved shoulder on the right.
    b) Only if a vehicle is turning left and you have a paved shoulder on the right.
    c) Whenever the vehicle in front of you is driving under 40 km/h.
    d) Whenever you can do so safely.

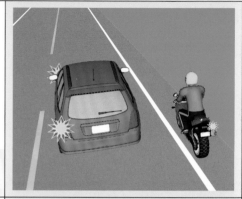

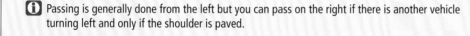

ⓘ Passing is generally done from the left but you can pass on the right if there is another vehicle turning left and only if the shoulder is paved.

248. **What tire track position should you be in if turning left from a passing lane into a passing lane?**
    a) In the left tire track.
    b) In the right tire track.
    c) In the centre tire track.
    d) It doesn't matter as long as you feel comfortable.

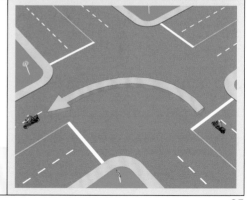

ⓘ When turning always ensure you have a blocking position so if you are turning from a passing lane into a passing lane, stay in the right tire track during the entire turn.

249. **Why is good traction important when driving on slippery surfaces?**
  a) To allow you to brake without falling.
  b) To allow you to balance without falling.
  c) To allow you to steer without falling.
  d) All of the above.

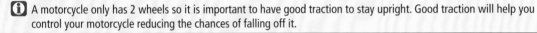 A motorcycle only has 2 wheels so it is important to have good traction to stay upright. Good traction will help you control your motorcycle reducing the chances of falling off it.

250. **What is important to remember about driving in fog?**
  a) Turn on your high beam light so you can see better.
  b) Stop anywhere on the road if fog is too dense.
  c) Reduce speed and turn on your fog lights if you have them.
  d) Speed up to quickly get through it.

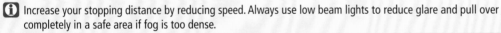 Increase your stopping distance by reducing speed. Always use low beam lights to reduce glare and pull over completely in a safe area if fog is too dense.

251. **What effect does cold weather have on tire pressure?**
  a) Tire pressure decreases during cold weather.
  b) Tire pressure increases during cold weather.
  c) Tire pressure stays the same during cold weather.
  d) Tire pressure can both increase and decrease during cold weather.

It is important to check tire pressure every time you get on your motorcycle but it is especially necessary to check regularly during cold weather.

252. **Why is the centre of a lane not a good driving position?**

   a) It is a good driving position because you are furthest from cars on either side.

   b) It is a good driving position because it is covered in gravel giving you better traction.

   c) It is a bad driving position because oil accumulates there and becomes slippery when wet.

   d) None of the above.

   (i) Oil from other vehicles accumulates in the centre of the lane making it extra slippery when wet and a bad lane position for motorcycles.

253. **What is black ice?**

   a) When snow is mixed with mud and then freezes.

   b) When newly paved roads are wet.

   c) When asphalt has a thin layer of ice on it.

   d) When ice is mixed with snow.

   (i) Black ice can form anywhere, especially on bridges which get extra cold air from below. This causes the temperature to drop quicker on the bridge forming a thin layer of ice.

254. **What are the affects of driving over grooves, metal gratings and scraped road surfaces?**

   a) You will experience a smooth and steady ride.

   b) You will experience an airlifting experience.

   c) You will experience the feeling you are losing control over your motorcycle.

   d) All of the above.

   (i) Whenever you are driving over road surfaces where it appears you may be losing control over your motorcycle keep a good grip on the handlebars and avoid sudden moves and overreacting.

255. If entering a freeway at what point should you turn on your turn signal?

a) As soon as you are on the exit ramp where freeway traffic can see you.

b) As soon as you are on the entrance ramp where freeway traffic can see you.

c) As soon as you are in the acceleration lane where freeway traffic can see you.

d) You are not required to use turn signals when entering a freeway.

ⓘ You want to be sure you are seen by other drivers so as soon as traffic can possibly see you on the entrance ramp, turn on your signal.

256. What does driving in "staggered formation" mean?

a) It means to stagger a group of motorcycles so they do not pose a threat to traffic flow or a danger to themselves.

b) It means to stagger a group of motorcycles across all available lanes so they do not ride closely to one another.

c) It means to stagger drivers far apart and increase their following distance.

d) It means to stagger drivers directly and evenly behind one another in a single line.

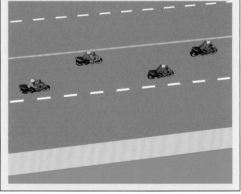

ⓘ In a single lane with the first driver in the left tire track, the second driver 1 second behind and in the right tire track, the third driver 2 seconds behind the first driver and in the left tire track and so on is driving in a staggered formation.

257. **How often should you check your mirrors while driving on a freeway?**
   a) Every 1–2 seconds.
   b) Every 2–4 seconds.
   c) Every 5–10 seconds.
   d) Every 15–20 seconds.

   ⓘ You can not drive on a freeway with your M1 licence but when you get your M2 licence and feel you have enough experience to drive on a freeway, perform traffic checks every 5–10 seconds.

258. **If a train is coming how far away from the nearest rail or gate should you stop when approaching a railway crossing?**
   a) At least 1 metre away.
   b) At least 5 metres away.
   c) At least 15 metres away.
   d) At least 50 metres away.

   ⓘ Never drive around or under gates and only proceed when gates have lifted and when it is safe to do so.

259. **What should you keep in mind at railway crossings?**
   a) Certain vehicles must stop at all railway crossings due to company policy so be alert.
   b) Approach parallel tracks in your direction at an angle of at least 45 degrees for best control.
   c) Slow down, use caution, look both ways, watch for signs, gates, lights and flagpersons.
   d) All of the above.

   ⓘ Also be aware that trains travel faster than they appear and they take at least 2 km to stop with full braking so do not think they can stop quickly to avoid you. Proceed only when safe to do so.

260. **Why should you not share lanes with other vehicles?**

   a) You are put at risk if vehicles are too close to you so sharing a lane should not be done.

   b) There is nothing wrong with lane sharing as there is safety in numbers.

   c) There is nothing wrong with sharing a lane because more attention will be drawn to 2 vehicles versus 1.

   d) Both b and c.

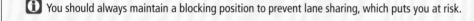 You should always maintain a blocking position to prevent lane sharing, which puts you at risk.

261. **Why is it a bad idea to shift gears while turning?**

   a) Your rear wheel can lose traction if too much speed is used which can cause you to skid.

   b) Your rear wheel can lock if you have a jerky downshift which can cause you to skid.

   c) Both a and b.

   d) It is not a bad idea to shift gears while turning as long as you proceed quickly.

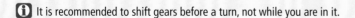 It is recommended to shift gears before a turn, not while you are in it.

262. What level should you keep cargo at and why?

   a) Keep it high to avoid a shift in gravity and to prevent interference with motorcycle balance.

   b) Keep it low to avoid a shift in gravity and to prevent interference with motorcycle balance.

   c) It does not matter which level you keep it at as long as you check it regularly.

   d) None of the above.

ⓘ Keep cargo low and balance weight equally on both sides. This will avoid a shift in gravity.

263. What should you do if you miss your freeway exit?

   a) Slow down, proceed to the shoulder, back up and get into the exit ramp you missed.

   b) Slow down, proceed to shoulder, turn motorcycle around and get into the missed exit ramp.

   c) Proceed and take the next exit.

   d) Proceed to the exit you missed using caution.

ⓘ Never back up or stop on a freeway if you miss an exit; instead, proceed to the next one.

264. If your motorcycle can handle towing a trailer what must you have in order to do so?

   a) A valid motorcycle licence.

   b) A valid motorcycle licence and a trailer permit.

   c) A valid motorcycle licence, a trailer that is registered along with a trailer permit.

   d) A valid motorcycle licence, a trailer that is registered along with a trailer permit and plates.

ⓘ Your trailer must also have the required white licence plate light and 2 red reflectors positioned far apart at the rear along with a red tail light.

265. What should you do if your wheels lock?

    a) Apply threshold braking.

    b) Apply speed through the throttle.

    c) Apply braking to the front wheel only.

    d) Apply braking to the rear wheel only.

ⓘ Briefly release the brakes if either wheel locks, then re-apply them without locking them. This is known as threshold braking.

266. What should you do if you are hit by flying debris or other things?

    a) Pull off the road immediately.

    b) As soon as it is safe, pull off the road immediately.

    c) Hold the handlebars steadily and keep looking at the road.

    d) Both b and c.

ⓘ Even if you have face protection you could have something hit you in the eye. Do not swerve to get off the roadway. Hold handlebars firmly and keep your eyes on the road. Pull off the road when safe and assess or repair any damage.

267. What should you do if your throttle gets stuck?

    a) Increase speed using the throttle, pull clutch in and shut off engine with the kill switch.

    b) Ease up on the throttle, pull clutch in and shut off the engine with the kill switch.

    c) Ease up on the throttle and pull in the clutch.

    d) None of the above.

ⓘ If you do not have a kill switch, pull the clutch in, ride it out and when stopped turn off the ignition with the key or stop the engine by braking. Braking hard is another option.

268. **What are some causes of wobbling?**

   a) Wheel bearings becoming loose.

   b) Spokes becoming loose.

   c) Steering parts becoming worn.

   d) All of the above.

   ⓘ Whatever the case may be, ensure you drive steadily while slowing down and keeping a firm grip on the handlebars; do not accelerate.

269. **If your engine locks or freezes what should you do?**

   a) Pull over and add oil to the engine when the engine has cooled.

   b) Pull over and add gas line antifreeze to the engine when the engine has cooled.

   c) Fill up the windshield wiper fluid.

   d) Fill up the gas tank.

   ⓘ Regular checks and maintenance are critical for safe and proper motorcycle performance. This helps avoid problems that may occur while you are on the road.

270. **Before you register or renew your motorcycle registration what must you show proof of?**

   a) You must prove you have a helmet.

   b) You must prove you have a motorcycle.

   c) You must show that you have valid insurance coverage.

   d) None of the above.

   ⓘ Falsifying insurance coverage can result in a hefty fine, licence suspension or having your motorcycle removed from you.

271. **What should you try to avoid when starting on a hill?**

a) You should avoid stalling.

b) You should avoid rolling backwards.

c) Both a) and b).

d) You should avoid using the front brakes while starting the engine.

ⓘ To avoid rolling backwards or stalling, start by using the front brakes to support the motorcycle when starting it and shifting into first gear.

272. **What documents must you carry with you at all times while driving a motorcycle?**

a) Pink liability insurance card, driver's licence, and permit.

b) Only the pink liability insurance card.

c) Only your valid licence.

d) None of the above.

ⓘ You must present these required documents immediately to a police officer if asked. You do not have 24 hours to present them. Failure to do so can result in a fine.

273. **Are you able to carry passengers with an M1 licence?**

a) No. It is illegal to do so.

b) It is only legal if you have a moped.

c) You are able to carry passengers only on a moped at speeds under 60 km/h.

d) You are able to carry passengers only on a motorcycle at speeds under 60 km/h.

ⓘ It is illegal to carry passengers with an M1 licence and at no point in the licensing program are you able to carry passengers on a moped.

274. **What type of helmet offers the best protection?**

a) A full-faced helmet.

b) A half-faced helmet.

c) A three-quarter-faced helmet.

d) None of the above.

ⓘ A full-faced helmet provides the best protection. There are many styles and sizes to choose from for best comfort; the brighter, the better, enabling you to be seen.

275. **What 3 steps will help you drive safely over objects?**

a) Tightly hold the handlebars, curve to one side and slightly rise on the footrests.

b) Tightly hold the handlebars, stay on a straight course and slightly rise on the footrests.

c) Tightly hold the handlebars, curve to one side, increase speed slightly.

d) Tightly hold the handlebars, stay on a straight course and apply threshold braking.

ⓘ When steering around objects is not an option, you will have to drive over them. Grip handlebars tightly, maintain a straight course, and slightly rise on footrests. Apply a little throttle to lighten the suspension in the front end.

276. **If you change the colour of your motorcycle what are you required to do?**

a) Tell the Driver and Vehicle Licence Issuing Office within 6 days of the change.

b) Tell the Driver and Vehicle Licence Issuing Office within 60 days of the change.

c) Nothing other than ensuring your motorcycle meets safety road standards.

d) Book an emissions test with Drive Clean.

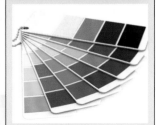

ⓘ Your vehicle registration has 2 parts; licence plate and vehicle permit. The vehicle permit must have an accurate description of your vehicle so anything that changes must be reported within 6 days.

277. **If you make modifications to your motorcycle what should you ensure first?**

    a) Ensure modifications are added correctly.

    b) Ensure the modification does not impact the safety or performance of your motorcycle.

    c) Ensure the modification meets Highway Traffic Act requirements.

    d) All of the above.

  ⓘ Carefully consider any modifications. Road race handlebars, for example, can impair your vision during shoulder checks and cause you to incorrectly assess your blind spot.

278. **What should you do if your chain breaks?**

    a) Firmly grip the handlebars to keep control over your motorcycle.

    b) Pull off the road safely and as quickly as possible.

    c) Both a and b.

    d) None of the above.

  ⓘ A chain that has been stretched may break and cause you to skid. Keep control of your motorcycle and pull off the road safely as soon as you can.

279. **What is key in making a quick turn or swerve in order to avoid a collision?**

    a) Quickly lean your motorcycle and proceed to turn in the direction you want to go.

    b) Slowly lean your motorcycle and proceed to turn in the direction you want to go.

    c) Increase the throttle and build more speed and then stop.

    d) Both a and c.

  ⓘ To avoid a collision a quick turn or swerve can be done by quickly leaning your motorcycle in the direction you want to go.

280. What effect can road race or clamp-on handlebars have on you?

    a) They can increase ability to perform good shoulder checks.

    b) They can decrease ability to perform good shoulder checks but can provide a tireless ride.

    c) They can increase ability to perform good shoulder checks and can provide a tireless ride.

    d) They can decrease ability to perform good shoulder checks and can cause you to tire easily.

ℹ️ While extra road race handlebars may look good, they decrease your ability to perform good shoulder checks. They may also make you tired and uncomfortable after a while.

281. What is included in registering your motorcycle?

    a) A licence plate and insurance coverage.

    b) A vehicle permit and licence plate.

    c) Insurance coverage and a vehicle permit.

    d) None of the above.

ℹ️ Ontario public roads require a licence plate on all vehicles on its roads. You get a licence plate, along with a vehicle permit, when you register your motorcycle.

282. Choosing a motorcycle safety course can shorten the amount of time you hold an M2 by?…

    a) 6 months.

    b) 4 months.

    c) 2 months.

    d) 1 months.

ℹ️ In addition to learning safety tips and proper driving techniques you will reduce the amount of time you must stay at Level 2 by 4 months.

283. If you are from another province can you drive your motorcycle in Ontario?

    a) As long as you have a valid motorcycle licence and you are at least 18 years old.

    b) As long as you have a valid motorcycle licence and you are at least 16 years old.

    c) As long as you have a valid licence and you are at least 18 years old.

    d) As long as you have a valid licence and you are at least 16 years old.

ⓘ If you are going to stay longer than 60 days you must then apply for an Ontario motorcycle licence.

284. When you have your M2, but preferably your M licence, and carry passengers how will your motorcycle react?

    a) Due to the extra weight, your motorcycle will react more slowly.

    b) Due to the extra weight, your motorcycle will react more quickly.

    c) Due to the extra weight, your motorcycle will react the same as with no passenger.

    d) None of the above.

ⓘ Your motorcycle will react more slowly because of the extra weight. Keep your distance and drive slower.

285. Why should you drive with your wrists low?

    a) So that you do not mistakenly decrease speed.

    b) So that you do not mistakenly increase speed.

    c) So that you do not mistakenly brake.

    d) None of the above.

ⓘ Proper body and hand position is essential to steering, balancing and maintaining speed on a motorcycle. Keeping your wrists low also enables you to reach the front brake lever more easily due to the position of your hand.

286. **What's the minimum depth of tire tread you should have on your motorcycle tires?**
    a) 4.5 mm.
    b) 3.5 mm.
    c) 2.5 mm.
    d) 1.5 mm.

ⓘ Improper tire tread will negatively impact your braking ability and traction on slippery roads. Ensure tire tread is even and at least 1.5 mm for best braking.

287. **Besides specific daily checks, what things should you also check weekly on your motorcycle?**
    a) Wheels and rims, shock absorbers, tire tread, brakes, the chain and all hardware.
    b) Wheels and rims, shock absorbers, tire tread, brakes, the radio and all hardware.
    c) Wheels and rims, shock absorbers, body paint, brakes, the radio and all hardware.
    d) Wheels and rims, shock absorbers, body paint, brakes, the radio and all software.

ⓘ Additionally, depending on the make and model of motorcycle you own, you should check the coolant and battery.

288. **Where should you shift your weight if the back tire blows out?**
    a) To the front.
    b) To the back.
    c) Do not shift your weight.
    d) Alternate between front and back.

ⓘ If the back tire blows stay where you are and do not shift your weight in order to maintain your balance.

289. **What can happen if you take a turn too fast?**

a) Your body will lean more than it should.

b) You can slide off the road and crash.

c) You may panic and brake hard, locking your wheels, slide and then crash.

d) Both b and c.

ⓘ Sliding and crashing are common when taking a turn too fast. Slow down and brake before turns.

290. **When you have your M2 but preferably your M licence and carry passengers what instruction will you give them about getting on the motorcycle?**

a) Get on once the motorcycle has started, sit as far back as possible, hold firmly to your waist.

b) Get on once the motorcycle has started, sit as forward as possible, hold firmly to your waist.

c) Get on once the motorcycle has started, sit as forward as possible, hold the handlebars firmly.

d) Get on once the motorcycle has started, sit as far back as possible, hold the handlebars firmly.

ⓘ You should also tell any passenger to keep their feet on the footrests and to lean when you do with the motorcycle, and to refrain from talking or moving suddenly.

291. **What should you do if you are being chased by a dog?**

a) Maintain balance and control over your motorcycle by not kicking the dog.

b) Kick the dog lightly to get him out of your way so you can focus on driving.

c) Do nothing as he will probably be outrun by you on the motorcycle.

d) Both a and c.

ⓘ Dogs may seem to pose a threat to you, but keep driving and focus. Alter speed to change the dog's tracking.

292. **What steps should you take when pulling off the road?**
   a) Check the road surface ensuring it is hard and good to drive on.
   b) Signal and check mirrors before pulling off.
   c) Find a far away spot off the road to rest so that other vehicles do not crash into you.
   d) All of the above.

ⓘ Leaving the road is a good idea if you have to check something or even to rest. Pull as far off the road as possible so others do not crowd your space or, worse, crash into you.

293. **As a buyer of a privately used motorcycle what must you get from the seller?**
   a) A Used Vehicle Information Package.
   b) The seller's licence plates and permit.
   c) The seller's driver's licence.
   d) A bill of sale.

ⓘ The package will include details about the vehicle for the buyer's benefit. The new owner of a used vehicle has to register their new vehicle within 6 days at a Driver and Vehicle Licence Issuing Office along with required documents.

294. **If driving on a freeway with 3 or more lanes which lane should you avoid driving in?**
   a) It doesn't really matter as long as you are careful.
   b) The passing lane.
   c) The centre lane.
   d) None of the above.

ⓘ The centre lane is not recommended as you will not have a blocking position. Choose a lane where you can best be seen that is far away from entrance ramps where vehicles need to merge onto the freeway or from exit ramps.

295. **What should you do if you encounter a large animal on the road?**
    a) Hit it head on to reduce skidding.
    b) Attempt to swerve around it.
    c) Jump off your motorcycle.
    d) None of the above.

ⓘ Try to stop in time but if you cannot, swerve around it.

296. **When pulled off the road and needing help where should you place your helmet?**
    a) Hang it from your handlebars.
    b) Fasten it to the back of the motorcycle.
    c) Place it on the road near your motorcycle.
    d) Keep wearing it so you do not have to put it on again.

ⓘ The signal to alert other drivers that you need help is to place your helmet on the road close to your bike.

297. **Why is it dangerous to slow down only by downshifting or reducing throttle?**
    a) It is not dangerous as this is how you should slow down.
    b) It is dangerous because your brake lights will not turn on.
    c) It is dangerous because other drivers will not know you are slowing down.
    d) Both b and c.

ⓘ You should always make your brake lights turn on to alert other drivers you are slowing down or stopping.

298. **If you are driving in the right curb lane which tire track should you be in?**
   a) The right tire track.
   b) The left tire track.
   c) In the centre tire track.
   d) You should not be driving in the curb lane.

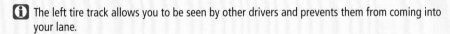 The left tire track allows you to be seen by other drivers and prevents them from coming into your lane.

299. **If you are driving in the passing lane which tire track should you be in?**
   a) The right tire track.
   b) The left tire track.
   c) In the centre.
   d) You should not be driving in the passing lane.

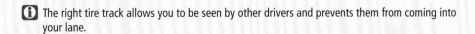 The right tire track allows you to be seen by other drivers and prevents them from coming into your lane.

300. What lanes should you avoid when changing lanes on a freeway, and why?

    a) You should avoid being in the lane next to an entrance ramp where other vehicles will be merging.

    b) You should avoid being in the lane next to an exit ramp where other vehicles may not see you and could cut you off in front as they exit.

    c) You should avoid lanes that you cannot easily merge into even though you may have your signal on early.

    d) All of the above.

ⓘ You should always ensure you are seen and that other vehicles do not come into your path.

301. How do you start a motorcycle?

    a) Turn on ignition, ensure kill switch is on, shift to neutral, set choke (if required), pull in clutch and press starter button.

    b) Turn on ignition, ensure kill switch is off, shift to reverse, set choke (if required), pull in clutch and press starter button.

    c) Turn on ignition, ensure kill switch is off, shift to neutral, set choke (if required), pull in clutch and press starter button.

    d) None of the above.

ⓘ When the engine starts, shift into first gear, keeping feet on the ground and easing up on the clutch as you move forward. Place feet on footrests, continuing to ease on the clutch. Give engine fuel by pressing on the throttle.

Practice Test Form

1. ❏ a ❏ b ❏ c ❏ d	21. ❏ a ❏ b ❏ c ❏ d	41. ❏ a ❏ b ❏ c ❏ d	61. ❏ a ❏ b ❏ c ❏ d	81. ❏ a ❏ b ❏ c ❏ d
2. ❏ a ❏ b ❏ c ❏ d	22. ❏ a ❏ b ❏ c ❏ d	42. ❏ a ❏ b ❏ c ❏ d	62. ❏ a ❏ b ❏ c ❏ d	82. ❏ a ❏ b ❏ c ❏ d
3. ❏ a ❏ b ❏ c ❏ d	23. ❏ a ❏ b ❏ c ❏ d	43. ❏ a ❏ b ❏ c ❏ d	63. ❏ a ❏ b ❏ c ❏ d	83. ❏ a ❏ b ❏ c ❏ d
4. ❏ a ❏ b ❏ c ❏ d	24. ❏ a ❏ b ❏ c ❏ d	44. ❏ a ❏ b ❏ c ❏ d	64. ❏ a ❏ b ❏ c ❏ d	84. ❏ a ❏ b ❏ c ❏ d
5. ❏ a ❏ b ❏ c ❏ d	25. ❏ a ❏ b ❏ c ❏ d	45. ❏ a ❏ b ❏ c ❏ d	65. ❏ a ❏ b ❏ c ❏ d	85. ❏ a ❏ b ❏ c ❏ d
6. ❏ a ❏ b ❏ c ❏ d	26. ❏ a ❏ b ❏ c ❏ d	46. ❏ a ❏ b ❏ c ❏ d	66. ❏ a ❏ b ❏ c ❏ d	86. ❏ a ❏ b ❏ c ❏ d
7. ❏ a ❏ b ❏ c ❏ d	27. ❏ a ❏ b ❏ c ❏ d	47. ❏ a ❏ b ❏ c ❏ d	67. ❏ a ❏ b ❏ c ❏ d	87. ❏ a ❏ b ❏ c ❏ d
8. ❏ a ❏ b ❏ c ❏ d	28. ❏ a ❏ b ❏ c ❏ d	48. ❏ a ❏ b ❏ c ❏ d	68. ❏ a ❏ b ❏ c ❏ d	88. ❏ a ❏ b ❏ c ❏ d
9. ❏ a ❏ b ❏ c ❏ d	29. ❏ a ❏ b ❏ c ❏ d	49. ❏ a ❏ b ❏ c ❏ d	69. ❏ a ❏ b ❏ c ❏ d	89. ❏ a ❏ b ❏ c ❏ d
10. ❏ a ❏ b ❏ c ❏ d	30. ❏ a ❏ b ❏ c ❏ d	50. ❏ a ❏ b ❏ c ❏ d	70. ❏ a ❏ b ❏ c ❏ d	90. ❏ a ❏ b ❏ c ❏ d
11. ❏ a ❏ b ❏ c ❏ d	31. ❏ a ❏ b ❏ c ❏ d	51. ❏ a ❏ b ❏ c ❏ d	71. ❏ a ❏ b ❏ c ❏ d	91. ❏ a ❏ b ❏ c ❏ d
12. ❏ a ❏ b ❏ c ❏ d	32. ❏ a ❏ b ❏ c ❏ d	52. ❏ a ❏ b ❏ c ❏ d	72. ❏ a ❏ b ❏ c ❏ d	92. ❏ a ❏ b ❏ c ❏ d
13. ❏ a ❏ b ❏ c ❏ d	33. ❏ a ❏ b ❏ c ❏ d	53. ❏ a ❏ b ❏ c ❏ d	73. ❏ a ❏ b ❏ c ❏ d	93. ❏ a ❏ b ❏ c ❏ d
14. ❏ a ❏ b ❏ c ❏ d	34. ❏ a ❏ b ❏ c ❏ d	54. ❏ a ❏ b ❏ c ❏ d	74. ❏ a ❏ b ❏ c ❏ d	94. ❏ a ❏ b ❏ c ❏ d
15. ❏ a ❏ b ❏ c ❏ d	35. ❏ a ❏ b ❏ c ❏ d	55. ❏ a ❏ b ❏ c ❏ d	75. ❏ a ❏ b ❏ c ❏ d	95. ❏ a ❏ b ❏ c ❏ d
16. ❏ a ❏ b ❏ c ❏ d	36. ❏ a ❏ b ❏ c ❏ d	56. ❏ a ❏ b ❏ c ❏ d	76. ❏ a ❏ b ❏ c ❏ d	96. ❏ a ❏ b ❏ c ❏ d
17. ❏ a ❏ b ❏ c ❏ d	37. ❏ a ❏ b ❏ c ❏ d	57. ❏ a ❏ b ❏ c ❏ d	77. ❏ a ❏ b ❏ c ❏ d	97. ❏ a ❏ b ❏ c ❏ d
18. ❏ a ❏ b ❏ c ❏ d	38. ❏ a ❏ b ❏ c ❏ d	58. ❏ a ❏ b ❏ c ❏ d	78. ❏ a ❏ b ❏ c ❏ d	98. ❏ a ❏ b ❏ c ❏ d
19. ❏ a ❏ b ❏ c ❏ d	39. ❏ a ❏ b ❏ c ❏ d	59. ❏ a ❏ b ❏ c ❏ d	79. ❏ a ❏ b ❏ c ❏ d	99. ❏ a ❏ b ❏ c ❏ d
20. ❏ a ❏ b ❏ c ❏ d	40. ❏ a ❏ b ❏ c ❏ d	60. ❏ a ❏ b ❏ c ❏ d	80. ❏ a ❏ b ❏ c ❏ d	100. ❏ a ❏ b ❏ c ❏ d

101. ❑ a ❑ b ❑ c ❑ d	122. ❑ a ❑ b ❑ c ❑ d	143. ❑ a ❑ b ❑ c ❑ d	164. ❑ a ❑ b ❑ c ❑ d	185. ❑ a ❑ b ❑ c ❑ d
102. ❑ a ❑ b ❑ c ❑ d	123. ❑ a ❑ b ❑ c ❑ d	144. ❑ a ❑ b ❑ c ❑ d	165. ❑ a ❑ b ❑ c ❑ d	186. ❑ a ❑ b ❑ c ❑ d
103. ❑ a ❑ b ❑ c ❑ d	124. ❑ a ❑ b ❑ c ❑ d	145. ❑ a ❑ b ❑ c ❑ d	166. ❑ a ❑ b ❑ c ❑ d	187. ❑ a ❑ b ❑ c ❑ d
104. ❑ a ❑ b ❑ c ❑ d	125. ❑ a ❑ b ❑ c ❑ d	146. ❑ a ❑ b ❑ c ❑ d	167. ❑ a ❑ b ❑ c ❑ d	188. ❑ a ❑ b ❑ c ❑ d
105. ❑ a ❑ b ❑ c ❑ d	126. ❑ a ❑ b ❑ c ❑ d	147. ❑ a ❑ b ❑ c ❑ d	168. ❑ a ❑ b ❑ c ❑ d	189. ❑ a ❑ b ❑ c ❑ d
106. ❑ a ❑ b ❑ c ❑ d	127. ❑ a ❑ b ❑ c ❑ d	148. ❑ a ❑ b ❑ c ❑ d	169. ❑ a ❑ b ❑ c ❑ d	190. ❑ a ❑ b ❑ c ❑ d
107. ❑ a ❑ b ❑ c ❑ d	128. ❑ a ❑ b ❑ c ❑ d	149. ❑ a ❑ b ❑ c ❑ d	170. ❑ a ❑ b ❑ c ❑ d	191. ❑ a ❑ b ❑ c ❑ d
108. ❑ a ❑ b ❑ c ❑ d	129. ❑ a ❑ b ❑ c ❑ d	150. ❑ a ❑ b ❑ c ❑ d	171. ❑ a ❑ b ❑ c ❑ d	192. ❑ a ❑ b ❑ c ❑ d
109. ❑ a ❑ b ❑ c ❑ d	130. ❑ a ❑ b ❑ c ❑ d	151. ❑ a ❑ b ❑ c ❑ d	172. ❑ a ❑ b ❑ c ❑ d	193. ❑ a ❑ b ❑ c ❑ d
110. ❑ a ❑ b ❑ c ❑ d	131. ❑ a ❑ b ❑ c ❑ d	152. ❑ a ❑ b ❑ c ❑ d	173. ❑ a ❑ b ❑ c ❑ d	194. ❑ a ❑ b ❑ c ❑ d
111. ❑ a ❑ b ❑ c ❑ d	132. ❑ a ❑ b ❑ c ❑ d	153. ❑ a ❑ b ❑ c ❑ d	174. ❑ a ❑ b ❑ c ❑ d	195. ❑ a ❑ b ❑ c ❑ d
112. ❑ a ❑ b ❑ c ❑ d	133. ❑ a ❑ b ❑ c ❑ d	154. ❑ a ❑ b ❑ c ❑ d	175. ❑ a ❑ b ❑ c ❑ d	196. ❑ a ❑ b ❑ c ❑ d
113. ❑ a ❑ b ❑ c ❑ d	134. ❑ a ❑ b ❑ c ❑ d	155. ❑ a ❑ b ❑ c ❑ d	176. ❑ a ❑ b ❑ c ❑ d	197. ❑ a ❑ b ❑ c ❑ d
114. ❑ a ❑ b ❑ c ❑ d	135. ❑ a ❑ b ❑ c ❑ d	156. ❑ a ❑ b ❑ c ❑ d	177. ❑ a ❑ b ❑ c ❑ d	198. ❑ a ❑ b ❑ c ❑ d
115. ❑ a ❑ b ❑ c ❑ d	136. ❑ a ❑ b ❑ c ❑ d	157. ❑ a ❑ b ❑ c ❑ d	178. ❑ a ❑ b ❑ c ❑ d	199. ❑ a ❑ b ❑ c ❑ d
116. ❑ a ❑ b ❑ c ❑ d	137. ❑ a ❑ b ❑ c ❑ d	158. ❑ a ❑ b ❑ c ❑ d	179. ❑ a ❑ b ❑ c ❑ d	200. ❑ a ❑ b ❑ c ❑ d
117. ❑ a ❑ b ❑ c ❑ d	138. ❑ a ❑ b ❑ c ❑ d	159. ❑ a ❑ b ❑ c ❑ d	180. ❑ a ❑ b ❑ c ❑ d	201. ❑ a ❑ b ❑ c ❑ d
118. ❑ a ❑ b ❑ c ❑ d	139. ❑ a ❑ b ❑ c ❑ d	160. ❑ a ❑ b ❑ c ❑ d	181. ❑ a ❑ b ❑ c ❑ d	202. ❑ a ❑ b ❑ c ❑ d
119. ❑ a ❑ b ❑ c ❑ d	140. ❑ a ❑ b ❑ c ❑ d	161. ❑ a ❑ b ❑ c ❑ d	182. ❑ a ❑ b ❑ c ❑ d	203. ❑ a ❑ b ❑ c ❑ d
120. ❑ a ❑ b ❑ c ❑ d	141. ❑ a ❑ b ❑ c ❑ d	162. ❑ a ❑ b ❑ c ❑ d	183. ❑ a ❑ b ❑ c ❑ d	204. ❑ a ❑ b ❑ c ❑ d
121. ❑ a ❑ b ❑ c ❑ d	142. ❑ a ❑ b ❑ c ❑ d	163. ❑ a ❑ b ❑ c ❑ d	184. ❑ a ❑ b ❑ c ❑ d	205. ❑ a ❑ b ❑ c ❑ d

206. ❑ a ❑ b ❑ c ❑ d	226. ❑ a ❑ b ❑ c ❑ d	246. ❑ a ❑ b ❑ c ❑ d	266. ❑ a ❑ b ❑ c ❑ d	286. ❑ a ❑ b ❑ c ❑ d
207. ❑ a ❑ b ❑ c ❑ d	227. ❑ a ❑ b ❑ c ❑ d	247. ❑ a ❑ b ❑ c ❑ d	267. ❑ a ❑ b ❑ c ❑ d	287. ❑ a ❑ b ❑ c ❑ d
208. ❑ a ❑ b ❑ c ❑ d	228. ❑ a ❑ b ❑ c ❑ d	248. ❑ a ❑ b ❑ c ❑ d	268. ❑ a ❑ b ❑ c ❑ d	288. ❑ a ❑ b ❑ c ❑ d
209. ❑ a ❑ b ❑ c ❑ d	229. ❑ a ❑ b ❑ c ❑ d	249. ❑ a ❑ b ❑ c ❑ d	269. ❑ a ❑ b ❑ c ❑ d	289. ❑ a ❑ b ❑ c ❑ d
210. ❑ a ❑ b ❑ c ❑ d	230. ❑ a ❑ b ❑ c ❑ d	250. ❑ a ❑ b ❑ c ❑ d	270. ❑ a ❑ b ❑ c ❑ d	290. ❑ a ❑ b ❑ c ❑ d
211. ❑ a ❑ b ❑ c ❑ d	231. ❑ a ❑ b ❑ c ❑ d	251. ❑ a ❑ b ❑ c ❑ d	271. ❑ a ❑ b ❑ c ❑ d	291. ❑ a ❑ b ❑ c ❑ d
212. ❑ a ❑ b ❑ c ❑ d	232. ❑ a ❑ b ❑ c ❑ d	252. ❑ a ❑ b ❑ c ❑ d	272. ❑ a ❑ b ❑ c ❑ d	292. ❑ a ❑ b ❑ c ❑ d
213. ❑ a ❑ b ❑ c ❑ d	233. ❑ a ❑ b ❑ c ❑ d	253. ❑ a ❑ b ❑ c ❑ d	273. ❑ a ❑ b ❑ c ❑ d	293. ❑ a ❑ b ❑ c ❑ d
214. ❑ a ❑ b ❑ c ❑ d	234. ❑ a ❑ b ❑ c ❑ d	254. ❑ a ❑ b ❑ c ❑ d	274. ❑ a ❑ b ❑ c ❑ d	294. ❑ a ❑ b ❑ c ❑ d
215. ❑ a ❑ b ❑ c ❑ d	235. ❑ a ❑ b ❑ c ❑ d	255. ❑ a ❑ b ❑ c ❑ d	275. ❑ a ❑ b ❑ c ❑ d	295. ❑ a ❑ b ❑ c ❑ d
216. ❑ a ❑ b ❑ c ❑ d	236. ❑ a ❑ b ❑ c ❑ d	256. ❑ a ❑ b ❑ c ❑ d	276. ❑ a ❑ b ❑ c ❑ d	296. ❑ a ❑ b ❑ c ❑ d
217. ❑ a ❑ b ❑ c ❑ d	237. ❑ a ❑ b ❑ c ❑ d	257. ❑ a ❑ b ❑ c ❑ d	277. ❑ a ❑ b ❑ c ❑ d	297. ❑ a ❑ b ❑ c ❑ d
218. ❑ a ❑ b ❑ c ❑ d	238. ❑ a ❑ b ❑ c ❑ d	258. ❑ a ❑ b ❑ c ❑ d	278. ❑ a ❑ b ❑ c ❑ d	298. ❑ a ❑ b ❑ c ❑ d
219. ❑ a ❑ b ❑ c ❑ d	239. ❑ a ❑ b ❑ c ❑ d	259. ❑ a ❑ b ❑ c ❑ d	279. ❑ a ❑ b ❑ c ❑ d	299. ❑ a ❑ b ❑ c ❑ d
220. ❑ a ❑ b ❑ c ❑ d	240. ❑ a ❑ b ❑ c ❑ d	260. ❑ a ❑ b ❑ c ❑ d	280. ❑ a ❑ b ❑ c ❑ d	300. ❑ a ❑ b ❑ c ❑ d
221. ❑ a ❑ b ❑ c ❑ d	241. ❑ a ❑ b ❑ c ❑ d	261. ❑ a ❑ b ❑ c ❑ d	281. ❑ a ❑ b ❑ c ❑ d	301. ❑ a ❑ b ❑ c ❑ d
222. ❑ a ❑ b ❑ c ❑ d	242. ❑ a ❑ b ❑ c ❑ d	262. ❑ a ❑ b ❑ c ❑ d	282. ❑ a ❑ b ❑ c ❑ d	
223. ❑ a ❑ b ❑ c ❑ d	243. ❑ a ❑ b ❑ c ❑ d	263. ❑ a ❑ b ❑ c ❑ d	283. ❑ a ❑ b ❑ c ❑ d	
224. ❑ a ❑ b ❑ c ❑ d	244. ❑ a ❑ b ❑ c ❑ d	264. ❑ a ❑ b ❑ c ❑ d	284. ❑ a ❑ b ❑ c ❑ d	
225. ❑ a ❑ b ❑ c ❑ d	245. ❑ a ❑ b ❑ c ❑ d	265. ❑ a ❑ b ❑ c ❑ d	285. ❑ a ❑ b ❑ c ❑ d	

Ontario Map

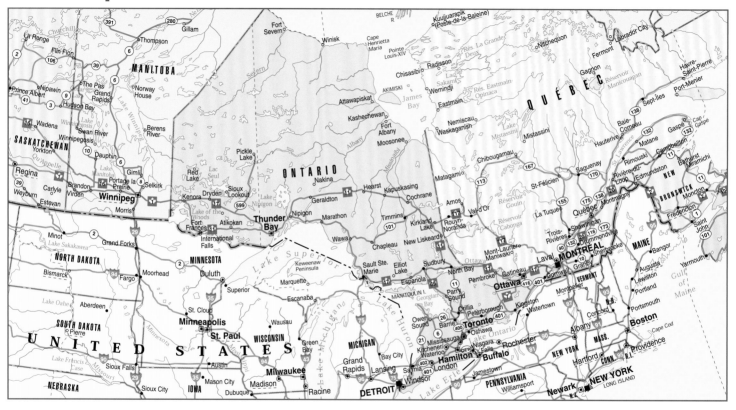

Customer Response Card

Thank you for purchasing this Motorcycle Licence Study Guide!

Our goal is to provide you with the information you need to pass Ontario Motorcycle driving tests.

Please complete the information below so we will be able to serve you and others better in the future. We value your comments and suggestions for improvements. Let us know what you think. Comments can also be e-mailed to: feedback@cccmaps.com.

(This information is for internal use ONLY and will NOT be distributed or sold to any external third party.)

Your Name: _____

Address: _____

City: _____ Postal Code: _____

Phone Number: _____ E-mail:_____

1. Age Group:

[ ] 16-24   [ ] 25-31   [ ] 32-40   [ ] 41-50   [ ] 51-70   [ ] 71-81   [ ] 82+

2. Where did you purchase your Motorcycle Licence Study Guide?

_____
(store name & location)

3. What did you like best about the Motorcycle Licence Study Guide?_____

_____

4. What did you like least about it? _____

_____

5. What would you add/change in the Motorcycle Licence Study Guide?_____

_____

6. Did you pass your applicable test after reading the Motorcycle Licence Study Guide?

[ ] YES   [ ] NO

7. Why do you think you passed or failed? _____

_____

8. Please provide any additional comments or suggestions you have: _____

_____

Fax or mail to:

Canadian Cartographics Corporation
70 Bloor Street East
Oshawa, Ontario
L1H 3M2

Fax: 905.723.6677

r.3

Canada's maps from coast to coast!

cccmaps.com

Visit us online to see our full selection of
road atlases, street atlases, pocket atlases, foldout maps, laminated maps and more!

Group Riding Tips

Riding in a group of 3, 20 or more is exciting, but can be challenging and even dangerous if you don't follow some common-sense tips. It's all about **communication** and **organization** to be **SAFE**.

Pre-ride Meeting

Start with a pre-ride meeting. Nothing formal; a 10-minute meeting in a coffee shop parking lot will do. There you will detail the ride plan (destination, route, stops, etc.) and discuss communication and group organization.

Hand Signals

Establish hand signals for stopping, whether it's for gas, restrooms, bike problems, etc. Communication can also be done electronically through CB, FRS, or GMRS radios. Ideally, the lead and sweep will have electronic communication.

Lead and Sweep

Identify a "lead" and "sweep" for the ride. The lead will set the pace and be responsible for knowing the needs of individual riders. Least experienced riders should be positioned directly behind the lead. The sweep is the last rider in the group, and keeps an eye on everyone ahead. The sweep communicates any issues to the lead, usually via radio.

Staggered Formation

All riders must ride in a staggered formation with a 2-second gap between them and the rider in the same tire track directly ahead. **If your group is too large, it's advisable to split into several smaller groups to allow other traffic to pass safely**

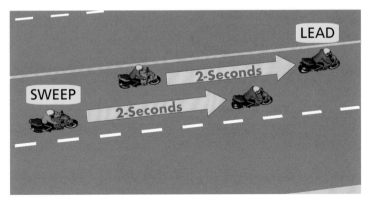

around you. **The time between groups doesn't have to be more than a minute apart.**

Meeting Place and Briefing

If your group will be travelling on multiple days, it's advisable to have a briefing meeting on each day of the ride. Pick a meeting place large enough and convenient enough for everyone to gather. The lead should conduct the briefing which includes all topics discussed at the pre-ride meeting.

Have Fun

Once everything has been discussed, enjoy the ride. If safety is kept in mind during the planning, organization and communication process, riding should be enjoyable, fun and group minded. *HAVE FUN*.

Answers to Study Guide Questions

Part 1 – Road Signs

Q	A	Q	A	Q	A	Q	A	Q	A
1	c	20	b	39	c	58	a	77	a
2	b	21	c	40	c	59	d	78	c
3	b	22	a	41	c	60	a	79	a
4	d	23	a	42	a	61	b	80	b
5	a	24	b	43	b	62	c	81	d
6	d	25	a	44	d	63	b	82	a
7	c	26	a	45	d	64	d	83	c
8	b	27	b	46	c	65	a	84	a
9	b	28	d	47	a	66	c	85	b
10	a	29	d	48	d	67	c	86	c
11	a	30	b	49	b	68	a	87	d
12	c	31	d	50	a	69	a	88	b
13	d	32	c	51	b	70	d	89	d
14	a	33	b	52	b	71	b	90	b
15	c	34	a	53	c	72	d	91	d
16	b	35	c	54	a	73	b	92	c
17	c	36	b	55	a	74	c		
18	d	37	d	56	c	75	b		
19	c	38	b	57	d	76	a		

Part 2 – Driving Responsibly

Q	A	Q	A	Q	A	Q	A	Q	A	Q	A	Q	A
93	d	112	c	131	c	150	c	169	a	188	b		
94	d	113	b	132	b	151	a	170	a	189	d		
95	b	114	b	133	a	152	c	171	c	190	b		
96	a	115	a	134	c	153	b	172	b	191	c		
97	d	116	d	135	d	154	b	173	d	192	c		
98	d	117	a	136	d	155	d	174	c	193	a		
99	b	118	c	137	c	156	d	175	d	194	b		
100	b	119	c	138	c	157	d	176	b	195	d		
101	a	120	a	139	d	158	a	177	b	196	a		
102	d	121	c	140	a	159	b	178	d	197	a		
103	a	122	a	141	d	160	b	179	c	198	b		
104	a	123	a	142	d	161	a	180	d	199	c		
105	c	124	b	143	c	162	d	181	d	200	d		
106	a	125	b	144	d	163	c	182	d	201	a		
107	d	126	d	145	a	164	a	183	c				
108	b	127	b	146	c	165	b	184	a				
109	c	128	a	147	d	166	b	185	d				
110	d	129	b	148	c	167	a	186	c				
111	a	130	d	149	c	168	a	187	a				